Everything Now
Steve McKevitt

route

First published by Route in 2012
PO Box 167, Pontefract, WF8 4WW
info@route-online.com
www.route-online.com

ISBN (13): 978-1901927-51-1

Steve McKevitt asserts his moral right to be
identified as the author of this book

Design:
GOLDEN www.wearegolden.co.uk

Support:
Ian Daley, Isabel Galan, Emma Smith
M Y Alam, Susana Galan, Tony Maguire,

Printed and bound by CPI Group (UK) Ltd, Croydon, CR0 4YY

A catalogue for this book is available from the British Library

Contents

In memory of Mike McKevitt
1944 – 2008

Part 1: Everything Now

Everything *pronoun*
All things

1. All things of importance.
2. The most important thing or aspect.
3. The current situation; life in general.

Now *adverb*
Immediately

1. At the present time.
2. At the time directly following the present moment.
3. Under the present circumstances; as a result of something that has recently happened.

Chapter 1
Everything Now

'You can never get enough of what you don't need to make you happy.' – *Eric Hoffer, philosopher and social writer*

What do you want?

Whether you are looking for motor cars, mobile phones, holidays or simply what to have for lunch, the range of options available to you can be genuinely overwhelming. With nothing more than a broadband Internet connection, you can enjoy immediate and unfettered access to millions of books, newspapers and magazines; thousands of movies and TV shows and almost the entire canon of recorded music. Many lifetimes' worth of content, all of it available at the click of a mouse. Whatever it is you want, you can have it. Everything Now.

We are living through a time of endless choices and unlimited convenience. We now take for granted the ubiquity of goods and services that can be instantly accessed, but the 24/7 society we live in – where everything is available practically all the time – is a recent achievement. Everything Now did not happen by chance or overnight. It is the culmination of a deliberate and concerted 30-year drive to increase choice and convenience for everyone. Those of us lucky enough to be living in the developed world today are, on average, healthier, wealthier, longer lived and better educated than at any other point in history. Our *needs* have been fulfilled and so, for the first time ever, we have an economy that is almost entirely devoted to the business of satisfying our *wants* instead. The question is: with so much effort dedicated to giving us what we want, why aren't we happier or, at the very least, worrying less and enjoying life more?

In the UK, levels of dissatisfaction with modern life were soaring even before the credit crunch of 2008. Two thirds of 15- to 35-year-olds, enjoying the highest living standards since records began, felt depressed or unhappy during these so-called 'best years of their lives'. When asked, fewer than half the British population agreed with the statement 'most people are satisfied with their lives'.

Modern life is not rubbish – for most ordinary people, it is arguably a lot better to be living today than ever before – but it is very expensive, requiring us to earn a lot of money to pay for it. In return for having Everything Now, we have to work harder and longer, so it's no surprise that unhappiness at work is often cited as a major cause of this broader discontent. There is a widespread feeling that the work–life balance is out of sync. 70 percent of workers claim that their job takes up 'too much time and emotional energy'. Around 65 percent feel stressed at work, with parents much more likely to be affected by this than childless couples. We are earning more than ever before, it's true, but access to consumer credit means that saving up for something has become anathema; instead we buy now and pay later. We may not be living beyond our means, but we are living ahead of them; our incomes never seeming to keep pace with things we are required to spend them on. In 2011, consumer debt in the UK stood at around £56,000 per household; a total of £1.45 trillion.

This is undoubtedly a compelling argument – that our unhappiness is a result of the amount of time we are forced to work to pay for the privilege of having it all – however, it is not the whole story. Working long hours is a symptom, not the cause of our unhappiness. Contrary as it sounds, it is Everything Now – through the very process of giving us what we want, when we want it – that is the primary source of our dissatisfaction. To succeed in a want-focused rather than a need-focused economy, companies and brands actually have to ensure that we are permanently kept in a dissatisfied state, from which the purchase of their goods and services will provide temporary, palliative relief.

The amount of time and effort going into convincing us that we are unhappy is truly remarkable. Consumers are hit with around 3,000 messages a day, almost all of which will be trying to persuade them that their lot will be materially improved if they buy this product, upgrade to that service or adopt another line of thinking. Everything Now makes us feel like we are in control of our lives, but the decisions we make are far from independent. We are permanently dissatisfied, always wanting something better, something we haven't got, and constantly nudged, cajoled, persuaded, coaxed and induced towards an ultimately ephemeral solution, whereupon the whole, unfulfilling process can begin again. The shocking result is that 80 percent of the things we buy are used only once and then discarded, usually leaving a slightly different hole in our lives that can in turn be filled with a slightly different product.

The impact of this can most clearly be seen where it matters most: family life. In 2007, a report published by UNICEF placed the well-being of UK children at the bottom of a league table of developed countries. In 2011, the organisation further explained this sorry position by suggesting that, as a nation, we have got our priorities wrong, replacing quality time with playrooms crammed full of expensive playthings.

Concluding that, 'Parents in the UK want to be good parents, but aren't sure how,' and that, 'They feel they don't have the time, and sometimes the knowledge, and often try to compensate for this by buying their children gadgets and clothes,' the report compares bottom-placed Britain with Spain and Sweden, respectively in fifth and second place. According to UNICEF, the key reason that these countries perform better is that these are places where 'family time is protected'. What our kids want is attention; what they get instead is materialism. Everything Now is geared towards providing the latter, but in doing so deprives us of the means to give the former: we might well have the money, but we certainly don't have the time.

One of the most compelling findings is that, 'All children interviewed said that material goods did not make them happy, but materialism in the UK seems to be just as much of a problem for parents as children... Parents in the UK often feel compelled to purchase consumer goods which are often neither wanted nor treasured.'

Perhaps an even more straightforward conclusion is that our children are unhappy because we are. Parents who work all hours to increase family income are naturally going to be too exhausted or too busy to give their children the attention they need and deserve; feeling guilty and attempting to compensate materially is an understandable response, but one that only exacerbates the problem.

Everything Now is an expensive, but effective, commercial cycle that is geared to satisfying wants: it can do nothing to address the needs of family life or personal well-being. The irony is that Everything Now indulges our whims and so we in turn behave exactly like spoilt children. We have become so used to getting our own way that, just as overly indulged kids, we get angry when we can't get everything we want, throwing tantrums if things fail to go our way.

Is this really what we want?

Chapter 2
We'll tell you what you want,
what you really, really want

'If there is any one secret of success, it lies in the ability to get the other person's point of view and see things from his angle as well as your own.' – *Henry Ford, founder, the Ford Motor Company*

In 1996, I found myself promoted to the lofty position of Head of Communications at Gremlin, which was, at the time, the UK's biggest computer and video game publisher. As is the way in British companies, my new role required me to stop doing what I'd proven to be good at over the previous four years – getting coverage for our games in the UK media – and to start doing something completely different without any training or experience: build and manage a team of people who could, in turn, get good coverage for our games across the whole of Europe.

It was a huge job and I realised quickly that if I was going to succeed, I would need to persuade other people working at other companies to help me. To do this I would have to convince them that any assistance provided would also serve their own best interests. Arranging these 'contra-deals' (a kind of marketing quid pro quo, where two entirely different products benefit from being promoted together, like cheese and crackers) was actually a major requirement of the job, so when a colleague in the sales department offered to set up a meeting for me with Intel's Vice President of Marketing in Munich – with a view to some mutual cross-promotion – I jumped at the chance.

Intel was, and still is, one of the biggest companies on the planet. Its primary business is the manufacture of microprocessors, the silicon chips that power most of the world's personal computers. Whether you're the owner of an Apple iMac, a Dell Inspiron or a Sony Vaio, the chances are that there will be an Intel chip inside. The business was founded in 1968 by two computing pioneers, Robert Noyce and Gordon Moore. Moore is a particularly important figure in the history of Everything Now. He is credited with the discovery of Moore's Law, which is in fact not a law at all, but rather the observation that computer-processing speed doubles approximately every two years. That's not to say it's not an important observation; Moore's Law has been the main driving force of economic and social change over the past forty years. It is directly responsible for all of the developments in digital electronics, computing and communications and, in so doing, indirectly for nearly every other segment of the economy.

In short, getting a meeting with the VP of Marketing at Intel was quite a big deal.

Eager to make a good impression, I spent several days honing my presentation. I focused on what I felt was important – an overview of the games themselves, some competitor analysis, a bit about the target audience – then I pulled out the key features and benefits that gave each title a competitive edge. I finished with a summary that highlighted why cooperation between our two great companies would be of enormous benefit to both of us. What I ended up with was, I felt, a punchy and persuasive case in favour of Intel helping to promote Gremlin's next raft of releases through its own marketing activity. And all in just 37 slides.

I met Manfred, the tanned and personable VP of Marketing, in the reception of Intel's opulent European HQ on the outskirts of Munich. He was an impressive figure, who had managed, I noted, to pull off that most difficult of looks, 'smart-casual'. We made small talk as Manfred guided me into a swish meeting room, containing a state-of-the-art AV system, which was furnished in a manner befitting one of the world's leading IT companies. I was heartened to see there was just going to be the two of us present. This made it feel more like I was there to negotiate a deal than to make a sales pitch, thereby pandering to my newfound sense of self-importance.

With hindsight, given the cosy nature of the audience, my pitch was overblown, overlong and overcooked, but Manfred was patient and respectful enough to make a few notes and politely asked a couple of questions.

In only 48 minutes, my presentation was finished.

'Thank you very much for your interesting proposition, Herr McKevitt. It was most useful,' said Manfred. 'Now if I may, I think it would also be helpful if I take you through Intel's business strategy for the next four years.'

Geez! I thought. Four years! I'd just whipped through four months of releases in around three dozen slides and three quarters of an hour – how long was this going to take?

As it turned out, I needn't have feared Death by PowerPoint, because Intel's business model couldn't have been simpler and Manfred had just one slide to present. He explained that Intel sold just three microprocessors, one at a premium price, one at mid-range and one at entry level. Every three months a new, faster microprocessor was introduced, which became the new premium model. The existing chips moved down a level, with the slowest one being discontinued. This pattern was simply repeated every quarter (and by implication ad infinitum). Each product had a total shelf life of just nine months: it was Moore's Law in action.

I had to admit, it seemed beautifully simple (especially when compared to the relatively convoluted manner in which my own company marketed and sold its computer and video games) but I did have one question. Manfred's model assumed that most people would upgrade their computers every three years. How, I asked, could he persuade people that they needed to do this? Manfred smiled, as if this was something he was expecting.

'It is not a question of persuading them that they *need* a new computer, but of persuading them that they *want* a new computer. Those are two very different challenges.'

He pointed out that most people changed their car every three years, even though there was usually no need for them to do this. Was it so unreasonable to expect them to do the same with their computers? I rephrased the question. How then, was he going to persuade them that they wanted to do this? Again he smiled.

'Why Herr McKevitt, I am not going to persuade them that they want to do this – you are. And others like you.'

Evidently delighted at my obvious bemusement, Manfred decided that it was time to enlighten me.

People do not buy technology, what they buy is functionality. Consumers do not purchase stereos, DVD players and mobile phones because they want the items for themselves, but because they want to listen to music, watch movies, and keep in touch with family and friends. The same is true of computers. But in this case there is much more functionality, so people end up buying computers for many different reasons – to work, play games, browse the Internet, edit movies, create magazines and so on. To do this they need to run software. To gain a competitive edge within a crowded market, software publishers were creating products crammed with features and optimised to run most effectively on the fastest machines available at the time of their release.

This was especially true for computer games, which, because of their rich graphics, placed the heaviest demands upon the hardware. If consumers wanted to derive the most functionality from the latest software – in the case of my games, experience the smoothest animation, highest resolution and most spectacular visuals – they would need the fastest computer, which would almost certainly contain one of Manfred's microprocessors.

However, as Intel's business model demonstrated, it would only be the fastest computer for a maximum of three months. The pace of this process was so rapid that Manfred could be confident that even the best computer available today would not be able to cope with the latest software being published three years hence. The pursuit of functionality – our games – could be used to force consumers to invest in Intel's new technology. Intel was not only creating faster microprocessors, it was also creating the demand for them.

Intel may be a master of the art, but it is certainly not the only company in the business of inventing wants as well as products. Manfred is correct: wants are very different to needs. 'Want versus Need' is one of the most basic concepts in economics. A need is something we have to have – like food, sleep or water. A want is something we would like to have – like a Big Mac, a Tempur mattress or a bottle of Evian. You might think that you cannot survive without your Blackberry or your BMW, but you can. It might even be the case that you do need a phone to carry out your work and a car to get around in, but what brand it is and, to a large extent, what features it has are really just wants.

Needs are rational and permanent. We have always needed – and will always need – food, water and shelter. The solution may change, but the problem is always the same, you can't create new needs. Wants, on the other hand, are emotional, ephemeral and ever changing. Just because you want something today doesn't mean you will want it tomorrow, always want it, or ever want it again. For example, back in 1981, everybody wanted a Rubik's Cube, it was the world's most popular toy, but it is unlikely to ever repeat this feat in the future. This transience creates an opportunity for anyone who is trying to sell us something – whether that's a product, a service or even an idea – and they can invent wants for us as well as the means to assuage them.

In 1976, a year with one of the hottest summers on record, almost nobody drank bottled water in the UK (unless they went on holiday 'abroad'); we spent less than £200,000 on just 3 million litres of the stuff. Today, each of us drinks an average of 33 litres per year, spending a total of £1.4 billion. We do this despite the fact that tap water is essentially an identical product that is as widely and freely available as it was in 1976.

Manufacturing wants for things like bottled water is what keeps us in a permanent state of dissatisfaction, because only by making us unhappy with what we have today is it possible to persuade us to pay for something that will make us happy tomorrow. In the case of bottled water, its success depended on us becoming dissatisfied with drinking tap water. The basis of this dissatisfaction is usually emotional rather than rational, it doesn't require hard evidence – all that is needed, perhaps, is promoting a notion that bottled water tastes better or using language to suggest it is somehow healthier than tap water. In Intel's case, the continual introduction of new microprocessors means that purchasing a new computer will only briefly appease the existing want for maximum functionality. Likewise, once upon a time, you may have yearned for an iPhone Mk1, but now, several upgrades later with that model nothing more than a distant memory, you've become dissatisfied with your current handset, and can't wait for the opportunity to forsake it for next year's version. It is simple and, as ever-increasing sales of bottled water, personal computers and mobile phones testifies, it has been extremely effective.

Maslow's Hierarchy of Needs is a theory of developmental psychology which describes the phases of human growth. It is often portrayed as a pyramid, with the biggest, most basic needs at the bottom (air, food, water), then safety issues (health, employment, property), moving up through relationships and esteem (achievement, confidence, respect), reaching self-actualisation at the top (morality, creativity and problem solving).

Maslow believed that these needs play a major role in motivating behaviours in Western societies where the individual is paramount. Basic biological, physiological and safety needs will always take priority over the need for respect or self-expression, but once they have been satisfied, the needs higher up the pyramid become increasingly important. As one set of needs is assuaged, focus moves to those on the next level up the pyramid. Everything Now is an extreme example of an individualistic society, hence our tendency is to be egocentric, focusing on the improvement of one's self and circumstances, with self-actualisation at the zenith.

Figure 1. Maslow's Hierarchy of Needs

For example, tackling obesity and associated issues of low self-esteem is a priority in the UK and USA, where food is cheap and plentiful, but in places where food is expensive and in short supply, these problems simply don't exist. There are few branches of WeightWatchers in the Third World and no need, at present, for Western governments to develop famine-relief strategies to feed their own people.

For almost all of human history, and certainly since the invention of farming, most people have lived short lives of abject misery. *The Road to Wigan Pier,* George Orwell's hard-hitting account of life in the slums of Britain (which is of course where most of the population lived at that time) was written in 1937, during the lifetime of many people alive today. Yet, while the world Orwell describes seems completely alien to us in the 21st century, it would have been all too familiar to our 18th- and 19th-century ancestors. The rapid improvement in living standards over the past 100 years has remoulded the aspirations of each generation.

All four of my grandparents were born during the early 1900s into poor, working-class families in Liverpool. I expect they wanted the same from adult life as their parents, which is not much more than paid employment, a roof over their heads, enough money to put food on the table and clothes on the backs of themselves and their children. My parents were both born at the end of the Second World War. Their wants extended higher, to a better lifestyle in which they might hold down a good job, own their own home, a car and a television set with enough left over to fund an annual family holiday. I was born in 1966. I wanted a university education, and a job that would pay me enough to afford my own home; a car for myself and my wife; several TVs, mobile phones and computers; at least two holidays a year and as many books, CDs and DVDs as I liked. Looking to the future, one wonders what the ambitions of the current generation might be. Is it as prosaic as accruing a greater property portfolio, a fleet of motor vehicles, granite work surfaces in the kitchen and 100" 3D, HD, flat screen, Internet-ready televisions in every room? Or perhaps we are in danger of running out of things to invent.

John Smart is the founder of the Acceleration Studies Foundation, a non-profit think tank in the US, which researches accelerating change. Smart believes that innovation is slipping out of view; literally occurring behind the scenes. Take computers or motor cars for example. Both look pretty much as they did a decade ago and operate in much the same manner, but a huge amount of innovation, development, computation and automation has taken place in the production process – nearly all of which is hidden inside the case, or under the bonnet. Smart says, 'Computations have become so incremental and abstract that we no longer see them as innovations. People are heading for a comfortable cocoon where the machines are doing the work and the innovating, but we're not measuring that very well.'

Yes we are still innovating, but we are doing so in small steps not the giant leaps we once were. Smart makes a very interesting observation about the areas in which innovation is taking place:

> Certain types of innovation saturation might now appear to be occurring because our accelerating technological productivity is beginning to intersect with an effectively fixed number of human needs... We may observe that as the world develops and we all climb higher on Maslow's hierarchy of relatively fixed needs, those who already have sufficient housing, transportation, etc, are now pursuing innovations on the most abstract, virtual, and difficult-to-quantify levels, like social interaction, status, entertainment, and self-esteem.

It is because we don't really need anything anymore that the focus of innovation has itself turned to addressing our wants instead. As Maslow demonstrates, once needs are taken care of, wants can be just as powerful drivers. This is all well and good if we know what it is that we want, but most of the time we don't. Nor do the things we want necessarily have to be good, either for ourselves or for the rest of society. Some people want to smoke, to take drugs or, as a more extreme example, to commit crimes. Needs require rational decision-making. However, the evidence is that decisions about wants are driven entirely by our emotions and these feelings can be so strong that they cause us to overrule or simply ignore rational objections. This combination makes us highly suggestible: easily persuaded by things that engage our sympathies, willing to be told what it is that we want, and then to act upon that information, regardless of the consequences. We should also consider that the people empathising with us – the ones engaging our sympathies and then telling us what it is that we want – are often trying to hawk us a solution as well.

You can find examples of this everywhere. Just look at an everyday product, like toothpaste. We need toothpaste to ensure our teeth and gums remain healthy. On average, people with healthy teeth live longer and tend to lead healthier lives than those who lose their teeth prematurely. Visit your local supermarket and you'll find around 120 different brands of toothpaste to choose from. Some promise fresher breath, others whiter teeth, others healthier gums. There will be brands for sensitive teeth, for people with fillings or cavities, there will be gels, pastes and powders, but despite this welter of options, each and every one will be virtually identical chemically; essentially the same thing, packaged and positioned in dozens of slightly different ways. The same is true whatever the category, from soap to soap operas. Scratch beneath the surface of Everything Now's apparently endless choice at any point and what you will find is hundreds of virtually identical products. Toothpaste is really just toothpaste.

Nobody needs to have 120 different varieties of intrinsically indistinguishable products like toothpaste or soap to choose from, and you may argue that nobody wants them either, but these 'choices' are offered in a much more subtle way. Where once there was a category called soap, now there are soaps for dry skin, greasy skin, sensitive skin; there is strong soap, gentle soap; soap in a bar, in a bottle, in a jar or from a dispenser; liquid soap, foam soap, hard soap, scented soap, simple soap, plain soap, soft soap and soap on a rope. Now all you have to do is choose one.

Things can't go on like this. And that's not some liberal cri de coeur, I mean it literally: they can't. Whatever your views are on climate change, you have to at least concede that we are not going to be able to rely on fossil fuels forever. If we carry on at the current rate of consumption – some 85 million barrels of oil a day, burning through the fossil record at the rate of 20 million years, every year – then we're going to run out sooner rather than later. Well, I'm all for screwing in low-energy light bulbs, buying locally produced peas and only drinking European wine, if that's what it takes to save the planet, yet I can't help thinking that, in the face of the thousands of freight carriers that are making their way to these shores slowly, but inexorably, from China and India to deliver their precious cargoes of Christmas cracker gifts and trinkets, these Herculean efforts might not suffice!

And even if we do discover substantial new reserves of oil and gas to ensure we can be supplied with miniature screwdriver sets and mini playing cards for the next 200 years, there still aren't enough resources for everyone to live as wastefully as we do in the developed world. We are currently using 1.5 times the world's gross annual product every year, which requires us to draw on an inevitably limited and dwindling stockpile of natural resources to make up the shortfall. But even as we burn through 50 percent more than we produce, over-fishing, over-farming, over-watering and deforesting as we go, competition for these diminishing resources is increasing as the huge economies in Brazil, Russia India and China (the so-called BRIC nations) and those in the rest of Southern Asia and South America become stronger. This means that even if those miniature screwdriver sets are still available, they're going to be a lot more expensive. And I do mean a lot more. Economists expect food prices to double in the next 20 years in real terms. Remember, this is the case even if we ignore climate change, which, I'll concede, is a bit like ignoring a herd of elephants in your living room.

Fear not. This isn't a depressing book about a post-oil apocalypse. I am confident – with good reason – that science can provide the solution to all these major crises, but by displacing innovation, Everything Now is making these huge, but potentially surmountable, problems much harder to overcome. We assume that the sum of human knowledge is endlessly increasing, but it is a mistake to think that we can still do everything we have ever done in the past. 50,000 years ago every man, woman and child on the planet would have been an expert stone knapper, able to turn a pile of plain rocks into finely crafted knives, axes and arrowheads. Today, aside from a few bearded enthusiasts and the odd paleo-archeologist, nobody knows how to do this. In 1969 a Saturn V rocket, the most powerful rocket ever made, took two men to the surface of the moon. We couldn't make that journey today – even if we could find the money to pay for it – because nobody knows how to build a Saturn V rocket anymore. Even the junior members of the Apollo programme are now comfortably beyond retirement age, while any of the seniors who are still alive will be well into their nineties. The plans and blueprints for the Apollo missions were never stored on a computer and NASA can't find the paper versions. It believes they were thrown out by mistake when it moved offices during the 1980s.

We live in the moment, tending to acquire only the information and skills we require to get us through everyday life. We no longer need to hunt for our food, so we've forgotten how to do it. As long as we never need that expertise again, this does not present us with too many problems.

The world we live in today no longer needs either stone knappers or rocket-scientists. It requires people to work out how the music industry can make money from file sharing; how Sunday newspaper executives can convince new readers that 500,000 words of content is worth the price of a cup of coffee; how TV channels can survive without relying on advertising revenue. It needs marketers and creative thinkers who can persuade millions of other people that This Brand is exclusively for them, that the next version of this film/TV/video game franchise is really the best one ever, or that some website helps us get closer to the things we love. It needs people who can develop products that are slightly better than the previous version, who can identify tiny gaps in crowded markets, who can think up new ways to package, deliver or sell the same things. It needs people who can find innovative ways of managing finance, who can manipulate the money markets, exploit political boundaries and economic loopholes, who can persuade people to leverage their assets, or to liquidate, re-mortgage, plough-back or reinvest, or just to keep their capital moving. But most of all it needs people who can work out ways of getting all of the above to us as soon as we want it. And of course, we want it now.

Inventors are innovating as much now as they ever have, it's just that they are solving problems that won't necessarily be rewarded with patents. The inventors are busy doing other things. Not necessarily brilliant things either. For every iPad there is a Chicken Nugget – but both are, in their own way, elegant solutions to problems people didn't know that they had.

Everything Now is enormously wasteful: a huge and unnecessary drain on the world's dwindling natural resources. By skewing our motivation it has entirely displaced the process of innovation. This is the real cost of changing our focus to wants instead of needs. Everything Now is making it almost impossible for us to address any genuinely big problems we face in the long term. We are not just demand-led, but are busily creating the demands themselves. We have become so obsessed with inventing and meeting the wants of the individual in the short term that attention has become diverted from the real challenges of meeting fundamental human needs of the future: energy and food supply, changing climate, population growth and the sustainable use of natural resources.

Chapter 3
What Happened to the Future?

'If people take the time to cook beans and put them on toast, why shouldn't we cut the process for them?' – *Bill Johnson, CEO Heinz*

Everything Now has propelled us forwards at such a frantic pace that we forget how recently the technology we rely upon today was introduced. You might ask yourself where you would be without your mobile phone, broadband connection and SatNav, but the answer is, most likely, in 1995, 2001 and 2004.

Recently I watched the *Back to the Future* trilogy with my three children, all of whom were under the age of 12 at the time. The films tell the story of Marty McFly, played by Michael J. Fox, a high-school kid from 1985 who travels backwards and forwards through time, essentially sorting out a variety of family problems (with the inevitable 'hilarious consequences'). Marty's adventures take him to the years 1955 and 2015. The scenes set in the 1950s look and feel like a different world and here much of the comedy is derived from the anachronisms that McFly creates with his knowledge of the future. However, when viewed in 2011, the most striking thing is how much the section set in the 1980s looks like today (certainly far more than the one imagined for 2015 with its blue drinks, hover-boards, holograms, robots and computerised clothing). In fact, this main part of the film feels so contemporary that my kids had no idea that it was actually set more than 25 years in the past. They assumed we were watching something that had been made in the past couple of years. We can write this off as a singular example of the phenomenon John Smart identifies – change taking place behind the scenes – however, there is more to it than this; innovation is not only out of sight, but out of mind as well.

The period of rapid, highly visible scientific advancement experienced by those living through the middle of the 20th century has come to an end. The period from the late 1920s to the late 1960s is synonymous with the realisation of big ideas – nuclear power, commercial aviation, television, computers, antibacterial drugs – but none was greater than the plan to put a man on the moon. In 1969, technological optimism reached its peak. The fervour was almost utopian, stoked by scientific breakthroughs that were fuelling the Space Race and the Cold War and which seemed to be happening all the time. The Apollo 11 Mission, which culminated with a touchdown in the lunar Sea of Tranquillity on 20 July 1969, is still widely regarded as the pinnacle of human endeavour. If we take that moment as our centre point and, like Marty McFly, look at the world 42 years into the past and into the future, we will see not just what things have changed, but how the nature of innovation itself is completely different.

In 1927, Charles Lindbergh became the first person to fly solo across the Atlantic. It was an amazing feat. His historic trip took 33 and a half hours. Travelling by steamship, the next fastest means of transport at the time, the same journey would have taken several weeks. Had you been alive in 1927 you could have read about Lindbergh the following morning in a newspaper containing reports about yesterday's events (unlike today's press wherein stories consist mainly of speculation about things that are expected to happen later today). This is also the closest you'd get to live pictures of the event. Television was still very much at the prototype stage and at any rate many homes in the UK didn't yet have electricity, with the development of a national grid still some 20 years hence. Within a week you might find black-and-white newsreel footage starting to appear in cinemas. Unfortunately, you still wouldn't get any sound with your pictures, because the release of the first talking picture, *The Jazz Singer*, would not come for another six months.

Little more than four decades later, an estimated half a billion people worldwide watched live pictures of Neil Armstrong taking his small steps and giant leap. Millions watched on their own colour TV sets. Almost every home in Europe and the US had electricity, which in many areas was provided by nuclear-fuelled power stations. The 'Energy of the Future' was available now. Life expectancy was increasing, thanks in no small part to the use of antibiotics, and the World Health Organisation was embarking upon what would ultimately prove to be a successful campaign to eradicate smallpox, a disease which in 1967 alone killed 2 million people.

On 1 October 1969, Concorde took her maiden supersonic flight. The beautiful, gull-winged aeroplane was an Anglo-French collaboration based on the RAF's Vulcan bomber. It would offer ordinary, paying passengers the possibility of repeating Lindbergh's trip in just a tenth of the time. American and Soviet competitors took this European initiative very seriously. In the US, Boeing was so convinced that sub-sonic passenger travel would be rendered obsolete, it designed its newly introduced 747 'Jumbo' passenger-jet so that it could be easily converted into a freight carrier. Not to be outdone by the capitalist West, the USSR brought forward the maiden flight of Konkordski, its own supersonic passenger jet, the Tupolev Tu-144.

Given all the advances that had happened in just over 40 years, one could scarcely imagine how much of a giant leap forward mankind was going to take in the next 40. In its July 1969 edition, esteemed publication *New Scientist* declared that, in view of what was to come, the Apollo 11 Mission was itself merely a trifle, 'A matter of no greater moment than just peering into the high recesses of a trapeze act in the Big Top at a circus.'

Yet, if anything, the achievement of Apollo 11 seems even more incredible today than it did back in 1969. The entire development time – from President Kennedy's bold announcement that the 'nation should commit itself to achieving the goal, before this decade is out, of landing a man on the Moon and returning him safely to the Earth,' to actual lunar touchdown – was just eight years. There was virtually no computing power available at the time, so the team made the most of the complicated calculations using drawing boards and slide rules. The on-board computer itself had only 64 kilobytes of memory. Cork, hardly the most high-tech of materials, was widely used in the Saturn V construction. Even the grandly named Emergency Vehicle Evacuation System consisted of nothing more than a sturdy rope for the astronauts to slide down.

So we could get to the Moon in 1969 with essentially a few cricket balls, a Commodore 64 and some fronds of gardening string (just in case), yet today, lunar space flight is the opposite of commonplace. Indeed no one can say with any certainty when we are likely to return to the Moon. As for planetary colonisation, is it unreasonable to say that this won't be achieved in the lifetime of anyone alive today?

It's not just that there's no lunar space flight today: none of the big things we were told we could look forward to during the late 1960s and 70s have come to pass. My own childhood expectations included not just frequent visits to space stations and colonies, but a job in a paperless office overseeing robots and computers for three or four short days a week (or, if I failed my O levels, possibly in a windowless factory). I would be spending my copious leisure time, and largesse, on supersonic flights to exotic locations, accompanied by my wife who would hopefully be one of the test-tube-baby-clones of Raquel Welsh I'd seen reported in the *Daily Mirror*.

The future has not turned out as we expected, but just because we do not notice that things are changing does not mean those changes have not had a big impact on the way we live. The similarity that my kids and I recognised in the 1985 represented in *Back to the Future* is, in fact, entirely superficial. My children noticed that Marty McFly is dressed a lot like they are, but today everyone wears jeans, T-shirts and trainers; even their dad. Back in 1985 Marty's outfit would clearly have marked him out as a juvenile. My father was only around 20 years older than me, but I never once saw him wear jeans or a T-shirt in his life. And as for trainers, he wore shoes even when he was coaching the football team. In the film we can also see that Marty owns a personal computer, video game console and a personal stereo, but what we are really seeing is just the casing. We don't see what the technology inside can do (which is practically nothing in comparison with today's) and so we use our imaginations to fill in the gaps.

My kids see Marty sporting a set of headphones and notice the Walkman brand on an iPod-sized device, so they assume he's listening to a MP3 player, not a cassette player (in fact I'm not even sure if they'd know what a cassette was). The video game console he has in his bedroom looks a bit like their PlayStation 3, so they imagine that, once his adventure's over, Marty will kick back by playing *Little Big Planet* online with his mates just like they do, rather than some tawdry three-colour conversion of *PacMan*. They recognise a television when they see one, so they expect that a UK-based Marty would, like them, have access to hundreds of digital channels, countless hours of downloadable content, the iPlayer and Sky Plus, rather than the reality of just four terrestrial channels, three of which broadcast for less than eight hours a day. As for the PC, that means only one thing to my kids: the Internet (or even more specifically, in the case of my elder daughter, Facebook), certainly not a clunky MS-DOS interface operated by using hard-to-remember command codes.

There is no denying that there have been significant developments in computing and telecommunications, and we must recognise that the impact these advancements have had on our lives is enormous. Life is emphatically better than it was in either 1969 or 1985, but what we have ended up with is a different better than the one we expected. Gordon Moore may have set the ship a sail, but it was Ronald Reagan and Margaret Thatcher who set the course for Everything Now, by establishing choice and convenience as driving forces behind innovation.

Neither choice nor convenience provided the motivation for Apollo, Concorde, the National Grid, nuclear power or any of those other giant leaps of the past. We should consider that these initiatives were also publicly funded. This was possible because levels of taxation and public spending were proportionately far higher than they are today. As such, these ambitious projects were not fettered by the need to deliver a profit or a return to investors. In the case of Apollo, the audacity of the challenge itself was enough to galvanise public opinion. As President Kennedy said himself, 'We choose to go to the Moon in this decade and do the other things, not because they are easy, but because they are hard, because that goal will serve to organise and measure the best of our energies and skills, because that challenge is one that we are willing to accept, one we are unwilling to postpone, and one which we intend to win, and the others, too.'

There was no commercial value in going to the Moon (and ultimately there proved to be very little in Concorde either), but unlike the CEO of a global corporation, there was no requirement for Kennedy to provide any either. This should not be misunderstood as a rose-tinted call for the return of nationalisation. There was a massive downside to nationalised industries that far outweighed these notable and, in all senses of the word, exceptional achievements. It should also be noted they weren't born entirely out of altruism either. These innovations might not have a direct response to any transparent market demand, but they were a direct result of shadier demands made by the military. The notion of two megadeath armies coming face to face on the battlefield is a relic of the Cold War, as outdated a concept as nationalisation. The requirements of military spending have changed. Today's wars are fought against enemies who melt away into the crowd or the countryside. The threat may not be any less significant, but it is more difficult to argue that squadrons of Eurofighter Jets (a project initiated in 1971, which cost an estimated £37 billion) are the most effective means of combatting the urban and rural guerrilla armies that we typically find ourselves up against today.

Once the boom of the early 1960s ended, it became much more difficult to gain a mandate for public expenditure from a less affluent electorate. By the mid 1970s these grandiose government-funded projects were being curtailed. The Apollo programme was cancelled, while Concorde was delayed and delayed and then delayed again. Concerns were for the present rather than the future. Industrial strife, recession, the Cold War, the energy crisis and the Labour government's cap-in-hand appeal to the International Monetary Fund, ensured that the Britain Margaret Thatcher inherited as Prime Minister in 1979 was a moribund, parochial place. There was no choice and precious little convenience; instead we had conformity and enforced compliance.

If you wanted a telephone in 1979, you could only buy one from British Telecom, a wholly government-owned telephone company. There was essentially just one model of phone to chose from (albeit available in a variety of three colours), a single payment plan and a waiting list for installation that ran into months. You could also expect the kind of customer service that today will only be familiar to anyone making an enquiry to HMRC regarding their tax return.

If you wanted a car in 1979, you could buy one from British Leyland, a wholly government-owned motor vehicle manufacturer. British Leyland had been using the same processes and technology to make the same, truly terrible vehicles since the 1950s. The government also owned the entire public transport system; all the rail, air and bus companies; as well as the gas, electricity, coal and water utilities. At least nobody ever rang to ask if you'd ever thought about changing your supplier.

I was 12 years old when Margaret Thatcher won her first election. Growing up during the 1970s I remember having very little choice. My parents, like everyone else, sent their children to the local comprehensive school. Any evidence as to whether it was a good or bad school was entirely anecdotal, because its performance was not made public, but given that there was no alternative anyway, it hardly seemed to matter. The list of things to do or be interested in during the 1970s was not a very long one. For a start, there were no digital TV channels, no home computers, no video games consoles, no world wide web, no mobile phones, no digital radio and there were no CDs or DVDs either. While it's true that video recorders were available by this time, they were so expensive that nobody I knew had even seen one, let alone owned one, so their existence was as good as irrelevant.

In terms of what was on offer entertainment-wise, there was football, but this should not be confused with the multimedia extravaganza it has become today. In 1978 it was little more than a pastime, to be played in the garden on your own or in the street and the park with your mates. There were of course football cards, magazines and Subbuteo, but these filled a genuine void as the game itself was conspicuous by its comparative absence on TV: just two highlights shows were broadcast showing only a couple of matches each.

Likewise, while it's true that many people were passionate about music at this time, access was similarly limited. If your tastes extended beyond the Top 40, actually finding the records you wanted to buy was usually difficult and expensive. Owning 20 or 30 LPs would mark you out as a serious collector. You were unlikely to hear anything other than chart music on daytime radio, and serious music fans could pretty much forget about TV altogether. That left vicarious enjoyment of the medium through one of the numerous weekly specialist newspapers and magazines. It was by no means unusual to have developed a wealth of knowledge about, and affinity for, a particular band or artist, without ever having heard them play or sing a note. So much so, in fact, that actually hearing them – which today seems like a ludicrously unremarkable feat – would often be worthy of some genuine cachet.

Apart from football and music, the only other entertainment source of any consequence was television. The experts say that kids watch too much TV. I say, with dozens of dedicated channels, broadcasting exactly the things they want to watch – as opposed to things that their concerned, middle-class parents might like them to watch – who can blame them? They said exactly the same thing about my generation, when there were just three channels showing nothing more than a test card for most of the day.

Certainly, when set against the paternalistic ennui of 1979, the Everything Now of today feels like an outstanding achievement. Nobody wants to return to a time when the good things in life were effectively rationed, just as necessities had been a generation earlier. To a time when successive governments decided what our best interests were and took collective decisions on our behalf, to deny us personal freedoms, without consultation. After that experience, no wonder being offered a choice felt liberating. But the increase in choice didn't stop at broadening access to products and brands; soon we were being offered choices in every area of our lives.

Anything seemed possible. Greater access to higher education made the trappings of success seem more attainable, while greater access to finance made them seem more affordable. One-time privileges started to become an entitlement. We started to expect a university education, a year out travelling, glamorous jobs, beautiful homes, luxury cars and exotic holidays. We also expected a risk-free existence, wherein we could rest assured that our health, safety and welfare would be taken care of and taken seriously. We were told that we could wave goodbye to boom and bust and say hello to a society that would treat us as individuals with unique needs; where anyone can have their say; where everyone's opinion is important; where everybody matters and everyone can expect to have 'opportunities'.

Yet the consequence of this achievement is that innovation is now almost entirely the preserve of the private sector. In the past, innovation and entrepreneurism have often been synonymous, but now they are so almost exclusively. Today, research is expected to provide a return on investment, so it is usually followed by the words 'and development'. It is impossible to imagine the CEOs of Apple and Google – arguably two of the world's most innovative businesses – making a speech espousing similar sentiments to Kennedy. If they did try to embody these values, they would be advised to ensure they came couched in the language of commerce, otherwise they would find their shareholders getting very antsy indeed. And it's not just business leaders. Away from the commercial world, the leading universities, traditionally the bastions of pure research, are finding themselves under increasing pressure to move down the intellectually less rewarding, but financially more lucrative, research and development route. In September 2010, UK Business Secretary Vince Cable, a self-proclaimed progressive, urged British universities to do 'more for less' and said taxpayers should only back research that has a commercial use.

We no longer notice the process of innovation, so it seems less important to us. Public attitude towards science generally is much less positive than it was at the beginning of the 1970s. Many of the biggest TV stars of that time were scientists or academics, often eccentric and colourful, but proper scientists and academics nonetheless. People like Patrick Moore, David Attenborough, Magnus Pyke, David Bellamy, James Burke, Kenneth Clark and Jacob Bronowski had peak-time TV shows and were consequently household names. They were the Ants and Decs of their day. There was nothing dumbed-down about programmes like *Civilization* or *The Ascent of Man* either. Science was everywhere and everywhere we were being told that it was good. In contrast with Cable, in 1965 soon-to-be Prime Minister Harold Wilson echoed the sentiments of President Kennedy by promising that a new Britain would be forged in the white heat of technological development, thanks to his government's careful management of the economy along socialist principles. A key part of that strategy was to significantly increase access to, and participation in, higher education, creating new universities and polytechnics specifically to focus on applied academic and vocational subjects.

If Wilson and Kennedy sound as quaintly optimistic today as the notion of holidays on Mars, then that is as much a testament to our view of innovation today as it is to their outmoded economic thinking. Today the kind of gee-whizz inventions that might once have been presented to us on *Tomorrow's World* – a show with an unashamedly non-commercial agenda – are served up together with cash-flow forecasts and business plans for world domination on *Dragons' Den*. Today's arbiters of what constitutes a good idea are businessmen, not scientists. The market savvy, like Peter Jones, Alan Sugar or Theo Paphitis – all sharp knives in the drawer, to be sure – can be relied upon to turn a dime more often than not, but you would not expect any of them necessarily to put the greater human need at the heart of their businesses.

Everything Now is what you end up with when choice and convenience are at the maximum; when innovation is driven exclusively by market demand. The exploitation of an idea becomes more important than the idea itself. In Everything Now, no benefit is too small and no inconvenience too minor to be packaged as a compelling proposition. When Bill Johnson, the CEO of Heinz, announces the launch of a new product that is going to take the hassle out of making beans on toast – surely one of the world's simplest recipes – and argues, without irony, that its introduction is the response to an identifiable market need, then you begin to realise that any inconvenience at all is really too much.

If we focus only on what the market wants we end up making baby steps not giant leaps: not cities in space, but instant beans on toast. Professor Brian Cox, chair in Particle Physics at the University of Manchester, is one of the few popular science broadcasters who can claim to be a household name. He supports the view that innovation out of sight is also out of mind. Cox believes that the UK is already 'the world's most efficient scientific nation', achieving almost 12 percent of citations despite having just 1 percent of the global population and 3 percent of the available funding.

'We already do more with less than anybody else. Almost half our economy rests on investment in universities and science. Any PPE [Philosophy, Politics and Economics] graduate out of Oxford should understand it, but there are a lot of them in the Treasury and they don't seem to. The impact is huge. The main purpose of science is to make you think, to give you a sense of perspective, to place ourselves in the universe.'

The answer is not a return to grandiose, publicly funded and government-managed projects, but we have thrown the baby out with the bathwater. The days of doing things simply because they are hard are well and truly over: we do the things that make life easier instead. But just as 'easier' is not the same as 'better', so choice and convenience are not natural bedfellows. Everything Now is like trying to ride two horses at the same time: possible in theory, but not when they start pulling you in different directions.

Chapter 4
Available in Magnolia, Vanilla, Cream or Beige

'The bourgeois prefers comfort to pleasure, convenience to liberty, and a pleasant temperature to the deathly inner consuming fire.' – *Hermann Hesse, winner of the Nobel Prize for Literature 1946*

The view that increasing choice and convenience is entirely positive is now so widely held that you would be forgiven for thinking that it always has been so, but in fact it is a totally modern concept. Post-war society under successive, consensual governments, was paternalistic, protectionist and prescriptive. Critics called it the Nanny State. By today's standards we would have found living through this time to be a perplexingly stifling experience. From buying a pint of milk after 5pm to choosing which school to send your kids to, many of the freedoms we now take for granted simply didn't exist. Usually, there was no attempt to provide rational explanation either; that was just the way it was.

Not very long ago, for half the weekend and vast portions of the evening, much of the country was effectively shut down. There was a huge amount of resistance to extended opening hours, much of it organised. In these more secular times, pressure groups like the Lord's Day Observance Society sound almost comedic, but as recently as 20 years ago, they were wielding a significant amount of influence over policymakers. The view was that Sunday should be a day of rest – for everyone. And 'rest' did not mean 'entertainment' or 'fun' and it certainly didn't mean 'shopping'. It is largely due to the success of pressure groups like the LDOS that the Sunday Trading Act only became law in 1994. The act allowed buying and selling seven days a week for the first time and was the result of decades of lobbying by consumer groups and retailers. At this time there was no late-night, weekday opening either. Almost all shops closed at 5.30pm, while online retail was not much more than a glint in the eye of entrepreneurs like Amazon's CEO Jeff Bezos. Evening entertainment was similarly moderated. We had to wait almost another decade before the night-time was opened up for business as well. Prior to the Licensing Act of 2003, pubs and restaurants stopped serving at 11.00pm, while nightclubs closed at 2.00am.

Today, in contrast, we hear the language of choice and convenience used all the time and rarely in a negative context. Politicians will use it to support a policy idea. They might talk of the importance of 'parent choice' when it comes to selecting schools. Brands use it to support product launches. They will say that 'consumer choice' determined the decision to release this slightly improved version of an old favourite. Supermarkets use it to support their plans for increasing market share. They will tell us it is 'customer choice' that drives them to open new stores or to extend existing outlets. Media owners use it to support revenue-generating initiatives or commissioning decisions. They claim that 'viewer choice' or 'reader choice' is paramount in determining output and innovation. All of these choices will be inevitably supported by a similar commitment to 'making life easier' for parents, consumers, shoppers and viewers at the same time. It's as if the whole world has been specifically ordered and arranged entirely for our benefit; as if nothing could be more important to these politicians, brands, retailers and media owners than making sure our every want is indulged as expediently as possible, no matter how whimsical it may be.

But Everything Now is patently no Utopia. As we have seen, dissatisfaction with the pace and pressures of 21st-century living was high even before the crash of 2008 plunged us into the gloomy uncertainty of a recession. Endless choice has been subjected to a great deal of scrutiny over the past decade. It has sometimes been celebrated – most famously in Chris Anderson's bestselling *The Long Tail* – but more often it has been challenged. The findings in books like Barry Schwartz's *The Paradox of Choice*, or research papers such as 'When Choice is Demotivating: Can One Desire Too Much of a Good Thing?' by Iyengar and Lepper, suggest that less choice would indeed make us happier.

In essence this is due to the fact that with choices come decisions, and while people quite like the idea of the former, they are less confident making the latter. Endless choice makes people unhappy with the decisions they take, because it's easy to imagine that you could have made a better one. If there are thousands of mobile phones to choose from, you expect to find the perfect handset, and end up disappointed if you don't. There's plenty of information available to 'help' people make that decision, but often that just ends up leaving them more confused and less confident about the decisions they have taken. How do you know that you've bought the right car, opted for the right mortgage or are wearing the right pair of shoes?

Certainly, when one is confronted by burgeoning shelves featuring scores of different brands for something as anodyne as yogurt, then it's easy to concur that really, you can have too much of a good thing. But it seems unlikely that any of us would suddenly become much happier just because some shadowy arbiter was limiting the number of choices available to us – even if this situation was actually possible to achieve. Endless choice has its problems, but it is not the problem itself. Choice is only one half of Everything Now; the real source of our dissatisfaction is the relationship between choice and its often-overlooked partner, convenience.

The rise of convenience has been more insidious than that of choice. Achieving 24-hour convenience may feel like liberation from the tyranny of the clock, but it has not come for free. There is a simple principle underpinning all product development and it is called the Project Triangle. There are many variations on the basic model but the one that's important to us concerns the values of Quality, Time and Cost.

Product development success is measured by a team's ability to manage the three values, represented on the axis of an equilateral triangle. These values are linked inexorably and understanding this fact allows you to make judgments about the time and money you need to spend to deliver products of a predetermined standard.

Figure 2. The Project Triangle

The way that the Project Triangle works is very intuitive. Imagine that as you pull on one axis of the triangle, the whole triangle expands; as you push, the whole recedes. This means it is not possible to optimise all three qualities – one will always suffer. You can start with any value you like, but any decision you take concerning one value will inevitably affect the other two.

For example, the Time it takes to deliver the product affects its Quality and Cost. If you want to deliver a product quickly, you can still choose whether it's high or low quality, but those decisions will determine how expensive it is to make. In effect you have just three options: produce a high-quality product quickly, and it will be expensive; produce one quickly and cheaply, and the quality will be low; produce a high-quality product cheaply, and it will take a long time.

Achieving ubiquitous choice and convenience necessarily requires a lowering of standards. You cannot deliver a product to the highest quality, in the quickest time, spending the least amount of money. If you want Everything Now, the pressure is on to produce as many things as possible as quickly and cheaply as possible: the only thing that can give is quality.

Henry Ford, the father of modern capitalism, knew everything there is to know about the relationship between quality, time and cost. Ford's Model T is the most popular motor car ever produced, selling over 15 million vehicles between 1908 and 1927. The oft-repeated story goes that a few years after its introduction, Ford sent out a team of researchers to visit scrapyards around the USA to find out which parts were liable to malfunction. In time, his team submitted their report, which found examples of almost every kind of breakdown imaginable and concluded that every part − axles, brakes, gearboxes, crankshafts, cylinders, pistons and so on − was prone to failure, with one notable exception. The kingpin of every single scrapped vehicle was in perfect working order, with years of life left in it. With ruthless efficiency, Ford inferred that the kingpins on the Model T were far too good for the job required and decreed that in future they should be made to a much lower specification.

Like most stories about Ford, I'm pretty sure this one isn't true; it feels uncomfortably close to the legend for me. It has been taken variously as a negative example of hubris, or to illustrate the disregard big corporations have for their customers, but occasionally it is used positively as an example of inspirational design. Whether it's true or not is unimportant, because what it tells us about product development − and specifically the controversial notion of planned obsolescence − certainly is.

Planned obsolescence was a policy developed during the 1920s of deliberately designing a product with a limited life, so that it would either stop working or become obsolete. It was widely practised because it stimulated demand by encouraging customers to upgrade or replace items sooner in the buying cycle than they would normally. Fortunately we are protected from this kind of cynicism today, and in Britain planned obsolescence engineered into products is considered a breach of consumer rights. Yet most companies do maintain a policy of ensuring that their components are 'just good enough' rather than over-engineered. If a mobile phone is going to be stylistically out of date in 3 years' time with 90 percent of models to be found mouldering away in drawers or toy boxes after 5, is there any good reason why you should ensure that all the electronic components will still be working in 10 or 15 years' time?

There may be no 'planned obsolescence' in Intel's microprocessors – as anyone who's turned on an 'ancient' computer that is 7 or 8 years old and found it still working can attest – but certainly obsolescence is the key to the success of its business model, as anyone who's tried to get some current software to run on the aforementioned 'ancient' computer will also be able to confirm.

In Everything Now, companies are under pressure to maintain profits in the face of shrinking margins. There is much less margin in products than there used to be. In 1981, a 26" Sony TV and video cassette recorder cost £1,200 (the equivalent of over £3,500 today); an Apple III computer together with a monitor cost £1,995; while a Sony Walkman was around £150. Today's equivalents can be purchased for a fraction of those prices. Nor is this loss of value restricted to consumer electronics; you can now drive around in a brand new Audi or BMW for around £250 per month.

Thankfully for the manufacturers, globalisation means that production costs are a fraction of what they once were and shipping goods almost anywhere in the world is similarly inexpensive. Add in the fantastically cheap, high-speed, global communications (available to both companies reaching out to customers and customers who want to connect with companies) and we are now in a position where we can pretty much buy whatever we want, no matter where we are.

The drive to increase choice and convenience over the past three decades has allowed more and more areas of our lives to become colonised by commerce. Today it is so advanced that some form of commercial exchange occupies almost every area of human interaction. If we turn on the TV, tune in the radio, log on to the Internet, open a newspaper or magazine, or simply step outside the front door and take a walk, we will find enormous and ceaseless amounts of effort, energy, and money being expended in attempts to communicate with us. The message, almost universally acknowledged and reinforced hundreds of times each day, is that if we make the right choice, then some inconvenience in our lives will be assuaged, usually by purchasing product X or service Y, resulting in our lifestyles – if not our lives – being instantly and immeasurably improved. It can be applied to everything from ready meals and razor blades to mortgages and mobile phones.

There is no reason why choice and convenience should be mutually beneficial nor necessarily positive. Having choices involves making decisions and decisions have consequences. Whatever choice you make means you will suffer an inconvenience: if you decide to buy a Audi, you're missing out on a Mercedes or a BMW; if you have the ice cream, you'll be missing out on the cake. No matter how trivial these dilemmas appear there will be somebody willing to take advantage of the opportunity to try and provide a solution – why not have cake and ice cream – which in turn leads to further consequences – worries about putting on weight or an unhealthy diet – and further opportunities to provide another solution – low-fat cake and ice cream.

Despite the choice available, when it comes to actually making a decision, most of us go with the flow or follow the path of least resistance. We are happy wearing the same kind of clothes, watching mostly the same TV channels, listening to the same music, eating the same food, reading the same books and newspapers, enjoying the same kind of holidays and sharing the same ideas, ambitions and opinions, as everybody else. So there may be a huge variety of products and services available, but most of them are destined to founder. 85 percent of products launched into supermarkets each year will be discontinued within 12 months. 40 percent of UK businesses get absolutely no visitors to their websites at all. Over 80 percent of the music on iTunes – some 15 million songs – has not even been downloaded once. Amazon stocks tens of thousands of lines that have never been bought once. 52,000 novels are published in the UK alone each year, most will never be opened, let alone read. 70 percent of technology launches fail to recoup their research and development costs.

This is the sting in *The Long Tail*. We have the necessary finance, we expect to have a choice, products have never been cheaper to produce nor more convenient to get hold of, but only a tiny fraction of what's on offer is worth having. We may feel we have choice and convenience, but it is not really possible to have both. While we have achieved ubiquitous convenience, the apparently endless choice we experience is in fact an illusion. Yes, we can choose to abandon our old Blackberry in favour of the latest model. Yes, we can choose to have a razor with five blades rather than one with four. Yes, we can opt for a toothpaste that tackles tartar and stained teeth, rather than one that promises only to deliver fresher breath, and yes, we can even choose to have ready-made beans on toast. Making all of these decisions will cost us money, but what will we have gained? We'll still end up having to shave once a day; our teeth will remain in much the same condition; our calls and texts won't be any more interesting; and it's fair to say that we're unlikely to spend profitably the 90 seconds or so we saved in the kitchen by looking earnestly for a cure for cancer.

Everything Now gives the impression that power rests with the consumer – after all, we are the ones calling the shots and making the decisions. This notion is pandered to in the rhetoric of corporate communication: 'We listened to our customers and…', 'What our clients demand is…', 'This initiative is a response to the demands of our subscribers…' but we are like hamsters in a wheel running to a standstill; getting nowhere fast. We work hard, we spend hard, but our circumstances remain unchanged.

On the typically joyless occasions that I am required to visit a shopping mall, usually in search of school uniforms, shoes or seasonal outfits for my incessantly growing kids, I am always struck by just how many people are wandering around unencumbered by bags of shopping, clearly not looking to buy anything. It's almost as if they are there simply because they want to be. This is not that I don't find the shopping centre useful − I do − it's rather that, like my dentist's, it's not a place I choose to spend time in unless I have to. It appears that I am the outlier in this respect, because today, shopping is the second most popular recreational activity in the UK and US. It is bigger than going to the movies, theme parks, theatres, pubs, bars or concerts, participating in sport, and even watching sport − only eating out is ahead of it. We spend more of our leisure time shopping than ever before. What was once considered a housewife's chore has become a national pastime.

With such a boundless array of options easily available, over one million attempts to push a message to us each year, and such a concerted and eager effort on our part to engage with the process, one would expect us to be living a myriad of different lifestyles, with different tastes, appetites and attitudes. In fact, the reverse of this is true: we all live remarkably similar lives, state remarkably similar preferences, hold remarkably similar opinions and want much the same things. We are choosing magnolia rather than vanilla and cream over beige.

Everything Now does not mean infinite variety. The reason for this is that demand for convenience is the main economic driver, not demand for choice or innovation, as many people think. Capitalism creates competition, that much is true, but the purpose of a competition is not to create choice: it is to create winners. Everything Now is not the result of a competition to deliver choice through innovation, but of a competition to deliver convenience through innovation. What suffers as a result is quality.

The winners in this are not consumers but major brands and corporations as we make most of our choices from a very narrow range of options. We buy our computer software from Microsoft and Apple, our groceries from Tesco, Sainsbury's and Walmart, our books from Amazon, our music from Simon Cowell, while the Internet is brought to us by Google.

The actual choices we make are within very narrow boundaries. Take our weekly shop, almost certainly made at one of the big supermarket chains. Quite simply, supermarkets are only interested in persuading us to buy everything from them. Not just groceries, but home insurance, personal finance, mobile phones, newspapers, CDs, books, video games, magazines, DVDs, electrical goods, clothing, homeware, holidays, even kitchen sinks. We can only choose whatever they have decided to stock. The business objective for all big corporations, not just the supermarkets, is literally the removal of choice.

'Ah, but things aren't that bad are they?' I hear you say. 'The Internet is fantastic. Technology is marvellous. I love my Blackberry – it's brilliant. Yes it is convenient that I can carry an entire CD collection around in my pocket, but it's also really high quality and it wasn't cheap. And what about all the other technological advances we've made over the past 30 years? Things are pretty good aren't they?'

I wouldn't disagree that the world is a pretty good place and there are many things to celebrate; in fact I'd go as far as to say that for most people, this is the best time to have lived in human history. And I'll concede that there have of course been many major technological developments over the past three decades: mobile phones, video games consoles, personal computers, CDs and DVDs, email, Sky Digital, iPods, MP3s, flat screen TVs and of course the Internet.

Again, these innovations are not themselves the problem, merely some of the symptoms. Just take a look around. Our homes are filled with books we've never read, CDs we've never listened to, DVDs we've never watched, games we've never played, clothes we never wear, gadgets we never use. A third of the food we buy gets thrown away. We have second houses we don't live in, we pay for gyms we never visit, subscribe for services we never take up, upgrade technology when we don't need to and change our cars, computers and redecorate our homes, on average, every three years. All of this has to be paid for. By credit cards, loans or mortgages in the first instance, but ultimately by somebody's hard-earned cash. Yours.

Everything Now keeps us dissatisfied, yet we play a vital and complicit role in ensuring its continuation. Every day we are stage-managed into making superfluous purchases that make our lives neither happier nor easier. The evidence suggests that we are remarkably susceptible to persuasion and, to keep things that way, Everything Now rewards ignorance. We may well be educating almost half of the population to degree standard, but we have no idea how 99 percent of the stuff we use and rely upon every day actually works. Most of the time we only notice when things have stopped working. We rely on a small number of sources for information and routinely form concrete opinions based on only a tiny amount of information: behaviour that allows our thinking, decisions and choices to be manipulated and controlled. As the world has become more complex, we have in turn become more ignorant of how it works and functions. Moreover, most of us are completely unaware that this knowledge might actually be important.

Part 2: Ignorance of Ignorance

Ignorance *noun*

Lack of knowledge or information.

1. 'Not ignorance, but ignorance of ignorance is the death of knowledge'

   Alfred North Whitehead,
   Philosopher and Mathematician

Chapter 5
Knowledge Without Application

'University brings out all abilities, including incapability.' – *Anton Chekhov, Russian playwright*

The effects of Everything Now are not restricted to commerce, its impact has resulted in a significant change in the shape and aspirations of society as a whole. One of the more surprising areas where this can be found is within our higher education system.

For over three decades the policy to vastly expand student numbers has enjoyed cross-party support. While there are clear differences of opinion on who should pay for it, there has been a concerted effort to achieve the objective. Consequently, regardless of who's in government, the aim remains unchanged: to provide the UK labour market with a greater supply of highly-skilled, graduate workers; improving the nation's international competitiveness and ensuring long-term, economic growth. But given that gaining a university education has never been more expensive than it is today, and with graduate unemployment at an all-time high, it seems reasonable to question to what extent this strategy has been a success, or indeed, if it has been successful at all.

In 1985, I became the first person in the history of my family to go to university. The inspiration behind this decision was my father. As far back as I can remember, he had been running what could be described as a heavyweight marketing campaign to promote the importance and value of gaining a college education. He assured me that getting a degree would be both life-changing and a great experience. What he was much less clear about were the specifics of how it would change my life and what the experience would involve. This is because, like that of most of his background and generation, his understanding of full-time higher education was entirely vicarious.

My father was born in Liverpool in 1944, into a poor working-class family. He was bright, passing his 11–plus and earning a place at grammar school, but neither he nor his parents ever entertained the notion that he could go on to university. In adult life he became a quantity surveyor, after gaining the necessary qualifications courtesy of a seven-year slog through night classes at the local college of building. Despite the fact that he felt he owed everything to his education, he was no fan of learning for learning's sake. His view of academia was utilitarian: he never enjoyed it and certainly didn't see why I should either.

At the time my father was growing up, universities were undeniably elitist institutions. In 1962, the year in which he turned 18, there were 31 chartered universities in the UK, producing 22,000 graduates annually from a total student population of 118,000. At this time, being a degree holder would have made you an extremely rare commodity, especially if you were not privately educated. In the eyes of people like my father, receiving a degree conferred membership of an exclusive club; a symbol of intelligence and achievement to be sure, but also a first-class ticket aboard the gravy train. Whether this view was at all accurate is questionable, but when the time came for me to begin my studies, it was definitely anachronistic.

In 1985 there were 47 universities in the UK with a student population of 282,960 students, producing around 80,000 graduates a year. They were still elitist institutions, but it was now elitism based on ability as well as social standing. By the time I arrived at Sheffield to study Politics getting on a degree course had become a realistic goal for many children from traditional working-class families. There was as yet only 5 percent of the population lucky enough to secure a place – with a further 10 percent going to either a polytechnic or one of the higher education colleges – and the public schools were still hugely overrepresented, but much less so than ever before. Like me, tens of thousands of comprehensive-educated kids were also becoming the first students in their family.

In the mid 1980s, it still felt like something of an achievement to be able to say you were a student. With hindsight, it was arguably the best time to be an undergraduate as well. We had our tuition fees paid; we had grants rather than loans; we even received supplementary benefit to tide us over the summer months and housing benefit to help us with the rent. Graduating in 1988 no longer qualified you for membership of any elite, but it did make you feel a little bit special. Throughout my working life only a minority of my peers and superiors have been degree-holders. The same could not be said by anyone who graduated just six years later.

Between 1988 to 1994 there were several radical changes to way that higher education was funded and structured, which resulted in a significant increase in the full-time participation of 18- to 21-year-olds from 15 to 30 percent. The abolition of grants and the introduction of student loans in 1990 relieved the state of some of the onerous, financial burden of the old 'free education' system. In 1992, the Further and Higher Education Act extended the University Charter to include polytechnics and HE colleges, which removed any remaining elite cachet that a 'university degree' might have conferred.

The process of expansion and reform continued apace under the New Labour Government of 1997. Declaring its three policy priorities to be 'Education, Education, Education', the Blair Administration's stated aim was to get 50 percent of 18- to 21year-olds onto degree courses by 2010. This would be funded by getting students to pay their own tuition fees. In the event, the 43 percent achieved was somewhat shy of the target, but still represents more than a five-fold increase since 1985.

In just 25 years, higher education has been transformed from a privilege available to the few into a right of passage for the masses.

In 2010 there were 1.5 million undergraduates in the UK. I do not wish to sound unsupportive of this development. Unlike my father, I've no problem with learning for the sake of it. In my work, I have never been required to put into practice what I learned while studying Politics, but in terms of personal enrichment, it was an invaluable, life-changing experience. I am sure the same is true for a lot of students at university today. A great number will also appreciate that higher education adds to their earning power as well as to their life satisfaction, but this is certainly not true for everyone who attends and runs up a substantial amount of debt in the process. In my own case, getting onto a degree was almost an end in itself and obtaining an excellent qualification was not my primary motivation. I was far more interested in the people I'd meet and the extra-curricular opportunities on offer. It is debatable whether I'd have been as interested if those fringe benefits had come with a £40,000 price tag rather than for free.

While I've no wish to see a return to the dark days when only a tiny minority had access to a university place, I do think it's reasonable for us to ask what this expansion of participation in higher education is all for. Despite the fact that a much greater financial burden has been passed on to the students themselves, for the country as a whole the growth in participation has been a hugely expensive undertaking. The proportion of GDP spent on education rose from 5.2 to 5.9 percent between 1995 and 2006.

The debate around the increase in student numbers tends to focus upon whether there has been a decline in standards and whether the degree itself has been devalued in the process. However, the matter of whether a degree handed out in 1980 has the same intrinsic value as one handed out in 2012 is a red herring. Instead, the salient issues are simply ones of supply and demand – are we supplying the right number of graduates for the labour market – and of appropriateness – are we producing the right kinds of graduate to meet the needs of the labour market?

To discover if we are producing enough graduates, we need

to compare the number of graduates we are producing with the number of graduate jobs available. What we find is that we are in fact creating far, far more graduates than our economy needs – for every seven graduates we produce there is just one graduate job.

Moreover, this is not a phenomenon that can be linked to the crash of 2008 and the ensuing recession. Even before this happened, during what was the greatest period of economic growth in world history, the supply of graduates in the UK was growing seven times faster than demand.

Answering the question of the appropriateness of our graduates is a little more complicated. Here we need to look at the skills gaps. A skills gap concerns the difference between the skills needed on the job and those possessed by the people applying for them. For example, have prospective doctors been trained to treat patients effectively; are would-be plumbers able to fit bathrooms and central heating systems competently?

Perhaps more shocking than the huge oversupply of graduates is the fact that the size of the skills gap in the UK economy is enormous, accounting for around 2.7 million vacancies in 2010. In many sectors, skills gaps are the biggest concern for human resource managers and business owners looking to hire capable employees. Finding people with a degree is easy, but finding graduates with job readiness skills, which help them fit into and remain in the work environment is a big problem.

What's more, these skills gaps are not evenly distributed. Some sectors – business and financial services, real estate, public sector, publishing and telecoms – have very low skill deficits and enjoy very high candidate–vacancy ratios, but many areas of high economic significance – computing, utilities, retail, engineering and construction for example – have many vacancies that attract few or no appropriately skilled candidates at all. In many other sectors, even for the graduates with the right skills, the outlook is getting less than rosy as a result of the glacial pace of post-credit-crunch recovery. The number of final year students who secured a definite job offer during the annual Milk-Round recruitment process dropped by a third in 2009 from the previous year.

By any stretch of these criteria, you'd be hard-pushed to describe the expansion of higher education as a success. This double whammy is worth considering, because it looks very much like we've spent billions of pounds training young people for jobs that don't exist and leaving them poorly equipped for those that do. How has this happened?

One of the major social changes brought about by Everything Now is that people no longer measure success in terms of material possessions, but in terms of experiences. The status symbols of the 20th century – cars, homes, holidays, televisions, computers, mobile phones – have become ubiquitous and for young people in particular, have stopped being an aspiration at all. Their ambition now extends beyond the accumulation of material goods, not because they have achieved an inner nirvana or become ascetic in outlook, but because these goods have become so easily attainable. Comforts and luxuries are no longer regarded as rewards or occasional treats, but as the norm. When you can have Everything Now, what you want, more than anything else, is an interesting life: the accumulation of experiences rather than possessions. Where you're going and what you're doing is of more importance than what you drive or what you own. The most significant ingredient in making your life less ordinary is what you do for a living.

The most sought-after career destinations for graduates today are all in the service sector. In 2009, the top three most desired fields were teaching, the creative industries and marketing. The creative industries covers a range of economic activities, including advertising, architecture, art, crafts, design, fashion, film, media, music, performing arts, publishing, research and development, software, toys and games, TV and radio, and video games. The sector is undoubtedly of economic significance. Richard Florida, one of the sector's principle proponents, believes that 'human creativity is the ultimate economic resource', and that the advanced societies of the 21st century will become more and more dependent on the development of knowledge through creativity and innovation.

It is very easy to understand the appeal of a career in one of these creative industries. I feel very fortunate to have spent most of my working life within this sector and can confirm that it is indeed a very rewarding place to work. It is certainly possible to have a career in the creative industries, but it is very difficult to get into. Precisely because it is one of the most popular destinations for graduates, the number of candidates is vastly greater than the number of jobs available, often by a factor of several hundred to one. In 2010, 12.5 percent of 16–18 year olds were following creative-related learning programmes, but the creative sector accounted for only 2.4 percent of the workforce. For almost all applicants, the task of securing the job of their dreams will be a daunting undertaking and for most it will end in disappointment. Yet this has always been the case.

My own experience, some 25 years ago, is shared by many of my colleagues. Getting a foot on the ladder required talent, but also perseverance and certainly a willingness to work for free in the early stages. There were no obvious routes into the sector via education, so the best advice for candidates was to try and obtain a good degree in an academic field like English or History from a good university, and support that with as much relevant experience as possible. In my case, this meant bolstering my degree by working on the student newspaper; submitting articles to magazines, fanzines and the local radio station; and then writing dozens of speculative letters to companies I wanted to work for in an attempt to secure unpaid work experience.

Today, people with a similar desire to work in the creative industries have the opportunity to study a range of specialist and training-related degrees. Journalism, Advertising, Film Studies, Graphic Design, Video Games, PR, Marketing, Television Studies and many other exciting courses are all on offer at universities in the UK. Yet despite this, the advice to candidates from employers in the sector about where and what to study remains the same as it was in the 1980s.

The irony is that while it is very difficult to get a job in the creative sector, it is usually very easy to gain a place on one of the supposedly related courses. There are 52 universities offering degrees in Film Studies, 37 offering Cultural Studies and 66 offering Television Studies. In almost all these cases the university offering these courses is ranked outside the Top 50. There are currently 141 video game related courses on offer in the UK, but only nine are accredited by the industry body. In April 2011, Ian Livingstone, Life President of Eidos, the British video games publisher that created Lara Croft and Tomb Raider, described most video game degrees as, 'A waste of time, energy and money... not remotely geared to a career in the sector... What we need is people with computer programming skills, not people who've gained an understanding of the history of the genre.'

The choice to select a pseudo-vocational degree, with no real prospects of a job at all at the end of it, is really no choice at all. From the students' perspective, this seems counter-intuitive. If someone wants to be an architect they need to study architecture, if someone wants to be a doctor they need to study medicine, so surely it must follow that if you want to be a video game designer, then you need to get yourself a degree in video games?

A similar oversupply problem exists within marketing. PR is the most popular discipline in this field. There are 33 colleges offering dedicated degree courses in Public Relations, but in terms of jobs, less than 50,000 people work in PR roles in the UK and more than half of those are employed by organisations in the public sector. Yet here again, the best advice about how to secure yourself one of the rare graduate positions in the field is not to do one of the PR courses, but to gain a good degree in an academic subject from one of the better universities (none of whom offer PR courses) and to get as much writing and work experience as possible.

The key point is not that studying for these degrees is a waste of time. There is nothing necessarily wrong with undertaking a degree in PR, Media Studies or any of the other subjects mentioned, if that's what people want to do. Nor does it mean that if you study one of these degrees then you won't be able to get a job in the media or PR. The fundamental issues here are that these degrees do not necessarily lead to a job in the sector (so if that is your only reason for studying them, then you are probably better off studying something else) and moreover, that they don't provide training for the real jobs that are available either.

There are industries and niches with less appealing profiles, but with real growth prospects, where there are shortages of appropriately skilled people. Sectors such as engineering continue to struggle to attract better qualified young people. The Institute of Engineering and Technology states that only around half of its members are able to recruit enough people into engineering and technical roles. This lack of expertise has implications for us all, not just the businesses themselves. We currently have enough trained nuclear physicists to decommission the existing nuclear power stations, but there are not enough to design and build new ones as well. Meanwhile students with the ability to fill these roles are studying subjects that definitely won't lead to a career in the field. In 2009 there were 5,664 people studying forensic science, made popular through glamorous TV programmes such as *CSI*, but only 5,000 people in total working in the UK forensic science industry.

One might be inclined to blame the universities themselves but that is unfair. It is the system within which they operate that is at fault. The decision to supply the labour market with more graduates was taken without really considering what the needs of the labour market actually were. Historically, degrees themselves have never really provided specific training, rather giving students a grounding in deep analytical thinking as a means to understanding complex ideas and developing intellectual competence. Unsurprisingly, the role of educators has been to educate their students in the subject to the best of their ability, not to prepare them for jobs after they leave.

The introduction of league tables in the 1990s brought the universities under increasing public scrutiny. Regardless of the various issues surrounding the real value of league tables, they are the only comparative information source that parents and students have to go on, so they are now a fact of academic life. Moreover, an institution's position in the table has a major impact not only on its ability to attract quality undergraduates, but private sector research funding as well. The top third of the table is dominated by the universities that do the most research and which are therefore the best funded. For new universities especially, where access to research funding is limited, the focus has been almost exclusively on attracting undergraduate students.

There are also implications for the research culture in universities; institutions are now competing with think tanks, in both public and private sectors, and other consultancies outside academia for research funding. The strategic implications for universities themselves are clear. The Russell Group (i.e. 20 of the UK's top universities) acts as a sort of Premier League, competing for the most lucrative research contracts, which will in turn enable them to consolidate their position by attracting higher quality staff and undergraduates. The next group is looking to displace members of this elite. Its members are likely to have a small number of star performing departments that they will try to leverage in order to compete effectively. For the remaining 50 percent, lucrative research contracts are little more than a pipe dream, so they take a populist approach, attracting as many undergraduates as possible onto a range of 'vocational' courses.

For all the changes in legislation, and many billions spent, what we have ended up with is a pyramid with an extremely broad base. Within those institutions at the top are all the students who would probably have gone to university twenty years ago. From the middle to the bottom, we find all those who probably wouldn't have. The primary concerns for all colleges, particularly the new universities, boil down to the number of undergraduates they can attract and the quality of the degrees that they confer upon them. What happens to the students once they have graduated might be of moral importance to some individual tutors, but in practical terms it matters very little to the institution and indeed the results would tell us very little about the quality of either the course or the teaching.

It might not be the universities' fault – after all they were told to supply more graduates and that is what they have done – but I do think it is a scandal that so many young people are being hoodwinked into studying for expensive degrees under the auspices that these qualifications are the key that will open the door to a dream career. Institutions are understandably willing to train undergraduates, whether at government expense or funded by loans, regardless of the needs of the economy. Degrees in media or film are positioned to prospective students as vocational qualifications: a conduit to jobs in media or the film industry in the same way that dentistry or civil engineering degrees lead to careers in dental care or construction. Students are often blissfully unaware of their chances of gaining related employment in fields where the number of training places massively exceeds the real number of jobs available.

The cost of studying for a degree is likely to treble for anyone starting a course after 2012. Many people are likely to find that their degree will be the first, and worst, major purchasing decision that they are ever likely to make. Higher education will retain its reputation as a life-changing experience, but often it will be for all the wrong reasons.

The opening up of higher education has made the system more egalitarian, but the truth is, however it is structured, we will end up with a system where the brightest students will tend to study at the better universities and tend to end up with better jobs. The only real areas of discussion are: where is it sensible to draw the line and how can it be targeted more appropriately and marketed more truthfully?

The overriding structural problem has been the narrow range of Key Performance Indicators (KPIs) which are used to measure college performance: that is, qualification rates rather than rates of employment – and the quality of that employment – post qualification. In 2011 the coalition government put employability and skills at the top of the university agenda. In the context of commercial viability for all concerned, it will be beneficial to have a broader set of measures to recognise success in wider economic and job output terms as well, but for such a shift to be effective, the whole system requires an overhaul, as it is highly debatable whether a degree is even the right kind of qualification at all, outside of the traditional academic subjects.

The failure of the higher education system goes far beyond recruiting credulous students onto pseudo-vocational courses of dubious quality. The demand for those courses is being driven by the desire for an exciting career, which is in many cases unrealistic. Everything Now will make it extremely difficult to rein in this ambition. A generation used to getting what they want, when they want it, naturally respond positively when offered what appear to be exciting choices and opportunities, even though they are not the gateway to exciting lives and careers that they might seem. By gearing our universities entirely towards student demand, rather than commercial reality, we have inappropriately skilled a significant proportion of our adult population at enormous expense, both financial and emotional. Today we will find thousands of graduates working in shops, bars, restaurants and call centres. While there's nothing wrong with those jobs in themselves, you certainly don't require a degree to do them, a realisation that will no doubt resonate with the legions of college leavers who are having to rein in their expectations.

There is one other matter to consider in the failure of this supply-led approach to education. Despite the fact that we are educating almost half the population to degree standard, we are not getting wiser as a consequence. Knowledge is still valued but, as we will see, it is a kind of knowledge that is not always useful. As the world has become more complicated, so we have become increasingly disengaged from the processes that drive it.

Chapter 6
The Great Unknown

'All men are mortal. Socrates was mortal. Therefore, all men are Socrates.' – *Woody Allen, filmmaker. Example of a Deductive Fallacy*

On the 26 June 1864, during the final year of the Civil War, the *New York Times* editor, Henry J. Raymond, ran a famous editorial attacking the disingenuous propaganda generated by a group called the Copperheads and their supporters in the media. The Copperheads were a high-profile group of powerful Northern Democrats who opposed the war with the Confederacy in the South. They either owned, or bought up, many of the most important newspapers like the *Chicago Times* and *Metropolitan Record* (New York's Roman Catholic paper), which they turned into fierce opponents of Lincoln's Republican administration. Many Copperheads were virulent racists who specialised in hysterical rhetoric. They claimed that the war was being fought not to save the Union but to 'Free the blacks and enslave Southern whites'. They also claimed that Lincoln was a 'fungus from the corrupt womb of bigotry and fanaticism' and a 'worse tyrant and more inhuman butcher than has existed since the days of Nero'.

A moderate by nature, Raymond's editorial is a spectacular piece of journalism. Rather than fighting fire with fire, gainsaying and challenging the Copperheads' claims with counter-claims, he took the seemingly more circuitous route of appealing to public sentiment in an attempt to engage rather than to terrify:

> The American people are credulous. Give them a
> fact plain, probable and undisputed, and they readily

credit it. Give them a falsehood positively stated, and they believe it with almost equal readiness, even though it bears evidence of falsity upon its face.

And to such an extent does this popular credulity exist that a well-started and well-circulated falsehood stands little, if any, chance of ever being successfully contradicted... But this peculiarity of the American people is not a bad one – on the contrary, unabused, it is a good characteristic. It is part of the foundation of that principle of mutual confidence which is so necessary to business and society, causing men to respect and place dependence upon the word of each other.

But it is the persistent and malignant abuse of this characteristic of our people, which is fraught with such evil results... [This] is now the chief strength and resource of their allies and friends, the Copperheads of the North.

Information was in short supply in the 1860s. The industrial revolution created a huge demand for data, which the news barons of the 19th century – like Raymond, who founded the *New York Times*, and Horace Greeley, who founded the *New York Tribune* – were only too happy to fill. Inevitably run in the interests of the proprietor, the probity of the information contained within these newspapers was usually questionable at best. This issue really came to the fore during the American Civil War. For the first time there was a mass communication channel available for dissenters, so it was possible for them to convey their anti-government feeling to a vast audience. The Copperheads were arguably the first organisation ever to use the mass media as a vehicle to cynically manipulate and persuade an unsuspecting public towards a political end, but they were not to be the last. We may be educating almost half the population to degree standard, and with the benefit of global transport and communications we are undoubtedly a much more worldly population than we were in the 1860s, but we are not wiser. The truth is that we are still a remarkably credulous bunch and, as long as they are stated in the same plain and undisputed fashion, we'll still just as readily give equal credence to truths and lies as our 19th-century counterparts. This is due to a startlingly widespread lack of interest in how the world about us functions.

Just as Everything Now has developed as a consequence of our focus on wants rather than needs, so the nature of the knowledge we require to navigate our way successfully though everyday life has changed too. There is more information available than ever before: so much in fact that the sum total of human knowledge is now so vast that even the greatest polymath could only claim to understand more than a fraction of a percent. Yet, on a day-to-day basis, most of us need very little of it. The fact that we don't know where our food comes from, how our energy is produced or how medical treatments work, causes us no problems in the short term; as long as there are things to eat when we are hungry, heat and light when it's cold and dark, and antibiotics to make us better when we feel ill.

Of course we still value knowledge; it's just a different kind of knowledge. We respect people who know a lot about football, music, fashion or comedy (or even the private lives of minor celebrities) and these experts are a lot more common than those who know how the electricity or water supply operates and are conversant with all the incumbent issues involved. Ask most people a direct question about how gas is supplied or petrol produced and they will be flummoxed, but ask them about Arsenal's chances in the League, the colours of the season, or their views on a new movie or album and you'll find many who are insightful, informed and knowledgeable.

It may not be news to you that most of us know very little about how the world functions. After all, driving Everything Now is ostensibly the desire to make life simpler and easier, so most people can get through it without needing to know how anything works at all. What might be a surprise is the amount of effort and money that has been invested, over the past quarter of a century, in an attempt to address this dearth of knowledge. It is an endeavour that has been almost entirely ineffective.

In the 1980s, the science community in Britain became concerned that the public understanding of the field, and especially of the breakthroughs taking place, was inadequate. Its primary fear was that a combination of ignorance and misunderstanding was affecting the quality of decisions made in relation to the allocation of funding. This in turn made it difficult to retain the nation's best talent – the so-called 'brain drain' – and maintain Britain's position at the forefront of technical innovation. At a time characterised by high unemployment, reductions in public spending, civic unrest and a radical shift from a manufacturing to a service economy, British science was feeling threatened, cash-strapped and undervalued.

In 1985, the Royal Society – an ancient and learned body containing the greatest minds from a range of fields that acts as science advisor to the British Government – addressed these concerns in a report called *The Public Understanding of Science*. The paper identified the crux of the problem as the low value society placed on science. A committee of leading academics sympathetic to this view was also put together with a clear and simple objective:

> [To] Review the nature and extent of public understanding of science in the United Kingdom and its adequacy for an advanced democracy; to review the mechanisms for effecting public understanding of science and technology and its role in society; [and] to consider the constraints upon the processes of communication and how they might be overcome.

Their conclusions were that everyone should have at least some understanding of science; that this should be provided at school; and that the knowledge gained should be of practical benefit, empowering people to make better decisions throughout their life. The committee also emphasised the need for more science coverage in the media, and recommended that the communication of ideas should become a duty, and principle, of those undertaking research.

Momentum gathered when, in 1989, a survey was published in the science journal *Nature* that measured the level of scientific awareness among ordinary people. Members of the public were asked questions such as whether the Sun goes round the Earth or the Earth round the Sun, whether insects have eight legs and whether radioactive milk can be made safe by boiling it. They fared quite badly as a whole. Researchers were particularly surprised that, despite a high level of interest in science, actual knowledge among respondents was poor. About a third of those questioned believed that humans and dinosaurs had co-existed; 70 percent believed natural vitamins were superior to synthetic ones rather than identical; 35 percent believed that the Sun circles round the Earth, and almost half had no idea whether DNA was to do with stars, rocks, computers or living things.

These results supported the view of the newly formed Committee on the Public Understanding of Science (COPUS) and it was not long before it became an issue of political significance. In 1993 a government white paper called *Realising Our Potential* was published with the stated aim of achieving:

> A cultural change: better communication, interaction
> and mutual understanding between the scientific
> community, industry and government departments.

The way to accomplish this was identified as improving the quality of the communications themselves and also access to media channels between scientists and the general public. This was intended to be a symbiotic initiative, one from which both science and the general public stood to gain enormously. What actually happened was quite different.

The science community immediately began releasing what turned out to be a relentless barrage of apparently unrelated pieces of information. The misguided belief was that people would somehow absorb it all and then apply their new-found science knowledge to solve practical, everyday problems they encountered. It was a process remarkably unscientific in design.

One legacy of this policy is that there is a great deal of science coverage today in the British media. Not just tucked away in dedicated science and technology sections either, but across the board: science reporting now accounts for around five percent of newspaper coverage. Despite this apparent popularisation, the science community accepts that it faces problems with public understanding of science today that are even more significant than those it experienced 30 years ago.

Subsequent research has revealed that the strategy of COPUS was based on a number of misplaced assumptions regarding the way we acquire knowledge about the world and how this, in turn, informs our attitudes and actions. It seems that most of us function quite successfully on a very simple need-to-know basis, so while we cannot argue with the results of the *Nature* survey, we can say 'So what?' Outside of a pub quiz or a Christmas game of Trivial Pursuit, it's difficult to conceive of a practical, cultural or social situation where knowing the answers to these questions would confer any benefit at all. That's not to say that the information isn't worth knowing – it is – but that is, in itself, not a good enough reason for why you should know it, so most of us simply don't bother.

There is a procedure in neurological medicine called a cognitive function test (or a cognitive impairment test). It is used by doctors to determine whether a patient is suffering from dementia. The patient is asked a series of straightforward closed questions: What season is it? Who is the prime minister? Who is the current monarch? What is a marsupial? – they are also shown a picture of a rhinoceros and asked if they know the name of the animal. Finally they are invited to carry out a mental arithmetic exercise, such as to sequentially deduct 7 from 100 (i.e. What is 100 minus 7? What is 93 minus 7?).

Most people, whether they are suffering from dementia or not, get some of the questions wrong. Common errors include mistaking autumn for winter, not knowing what a marsupial is, failing to identify a rhino, and, most widespread of all after the election of May 2010, believing that the UK has two prime ministers. Sequentially deducting 7 from 100 is also a task many (including this writer) find difficult without the aid of a pen and paper, especially when under pressure. This does not mean that we are all secretly suffering from dementia (in this test it is the kind of wrong answer you give that is important) but it does illustrate how poor we are at retaining knowledge we find unnecessary. Few people will find that their lives are inconvenienced because they don't know whether it's autumn or believe that Nick Clegg is prime minister.

Even when we are engaged, we have a tendency to assimilate only as much knowledge as we need to meet our own individual circumstances and very little more. This information is rarely transferable. We may learn how to change a plug on an electrical appliance, but what the wires we are connecting actually do is of no concern to us, which makes the knowledge difficult to apply in any other circumstance. A more extreme example would be somebody suffering from chronic or serious illness, who develops an in-depth knowledge of their condition to near expert level, yet knows practically nothing that is applicable to any other diseases.

We are very happy to compartmentalise knowledge in a world where it is impossible to know everything. Doctors know about medicine, joiners about carpentry and farmers about farming – the rest of us get through life without knowing about any of this, but we're still able to get hold of antibiotics, furniture and sausages whenever we need to. The processes behind the production of them all are a mystery, which few of us are interested in uncovering.

The belief that increasing scientific knowledge would automatically lead to an increase in understanding has proven to be wrong. Knowledge and understanding is not the same thing. A little knowledge will inform our attitudes, but it will not necessarily make us more positive about science nor persuade us to change our habits. For example, almost everybody knows smoking is bad for you, yet millions persist in this patently dangerous practice. Likewise, you can tell people more about genetically modified foods, but it is just as likely to result in outrage and protest as it is in support and consent. A little knowledge really can be a dangerous thing.

The popularisation of science has increased public interest, certainly, but it has not succeeded in increasing our understanding of the subject, let alone our acceptance. Interest can easily manifest itself as misgiving and we are more suspicious of science than ever before, as those wishing to persuade us of the reality of climate change know only too well. Despite the evidence for human impact upon climate change being accepted by virtually all the scientific community as incontrovertible, almost half of US citizens and a third of those in the UK believe the threat to be either exaggerated or unproven.

Furthermore, increasing public interest has not only created a platform for the ideas of bona fide scientists, but for a host of para- and pseudo-scientists as well, hawking everything from crystal healing and aromatherapy, to fad diets and feng shui. You don't need a distinguished career in research to write a popular book or front a popular TV show. Whether it's the erstwhile 'Doctor' Gillian McKeith suggesting that analysis of faecal matter is a guide to nutritional enlightenment; or 'guests' on car-crash TV shows like *The Jeremy Kyle Show* being told that a lie detector test is '99 percent accurate'; or even the high-profile patron of quackery himself, Prince Charles, selling 'detox water' at five quid a bottle through his exorbitantly expensive Duchy of Cornwall brand; presenting hokum as scientific fact is always manipulative and rarely harmless.

If the return of the snake-oil peddlers is a cause of confusion, then the situation is complicated by the damage that misleading, government-supported campaigns have done to public trust. In 2000, the British government shamefully took an equivocal position on the findings of a study by former surgeon and medical researcher Andrew Wakefield. His paper, entitled 'Enterocolitis in Children with Developmental Disorders', wrongly and fraudulently linked autism with the MMR vaccine. Rather than offer reassurance or guidance, the prime minister himself, Tony Blair, said that it was up to parents to decide for themselves whether they should get their children immunised or not. This advice led to a fall in the level of vaccinations, which resulted not only in a significant increase in entirely preventable cases of measles, mumps and rubella, but also jeopardised the immunisation programme as a whole by leaving too small a group vaccinated to combat an epidemic effectively. Remember these are childhood diseases, not childlike or mild diseases: measles, in particular, is a terrible illness causing blindness, deafness and even death in some cases.

Knowledge and trust are bound together indivisibly where the public appetite for information is concerned. As we have seen, the number of messages each of us receives each day is around 3,000. Consequently we have become extremely adept at filtering out information that doesn't engage us. Just because you are sending out a message doesn't mean that the public will consume it. Conversely, there are people whose view of climate change is based entirely upon what they have been told by Jeremy Clarkson. Clarkson's columns and books are widely read – far more widely read than all the world's leading scientific journals combined

– and he makes popular TV shows that reach an audience of millions every week. How much research he's done to formulate his position on climate change I couldn't tell you, but to me, his conclusions seem to be remarkably close to what he'd have liked to believe was true before his investigation started.

In summary, Clarkson is of the opinion that the case for man-made climate change is nonsense, and that oil will go on, if not forever, then at least until we've discovered a way of making hydrogen to replace it, so there's no need for anyone to moderate their behaviour at all. It's a position that seems to be based more on faith than on reason, but one that resonates strongly with frightened readers and viewers who would similarly like it to be true, and find it reassuring that someone in such a lofty position is so certain that everything will be okay. Geez! I'd love Jeremy Clarkson to be right, the problem is just that I don't imagine for a second that he is, on the basis that evidence points to the contrary.

What we find is that when the public does demand information, it is usually when they feel their trust has been betrayed, and they do this, not with open minds, but from a position of having actively constructed their own discrete areas of ignorance and expertise, based upon gobbets of information of variable quality and probity. Single, unrelated issues linked only by the fact that the people think they are important can have a galvanising effect, as the public becomes mobilised and loudly expresses its collective opinion.

This campaigning public is very different to the accepting public, wide-eyed and open-mouthed, that marvelled at phones with built-in cameras, wondered at 3D TV and gobbled up the Atkins Diet. They may not know what season we're in, or to which infraclass of mammal a kangaroo belongs, but collectively, armed with an opinion and some of the facts, they can prove a formidable opponent. Moreover, in these times of user-generated media, when it seems we are invited to 'have our say' every five minutes, there are many channels available for them to broadcast their dissent.

And so we discover that telling people about genetics does

not make them any more accepting of genetically modified food; that demonstrating the benefits of stem-cell treatments does not make them more supportive of embryo research; and explaining the painstaking legal process that goes into proving the efficacy of every new drug does not make people any less irate that the latest, highly expensive but inconclusively proven anti-cancer medication test is not available to people living in their postcode. Everything Now is not just the demand for convenience or for an easy and interesting life: it is the demand for things to 'go our way'. The universe may not revolve around us, but as the comedian Daniel Kitson points out, from where we're standing, it very much looks like it does.

As the world has become more complicated we have become disengaged from an increasing number of processes and forces that make our lifestyle possible. Instead, our focus is upon living our own lives as successfully as we can. Which brings us to yet another contradiction of Everything Now: the population is better educated than ever before and there is more information available than ever before, but it is no less credulous or ignorant as a result. Furthermore, because of our education, because of the availability of information, and because of the multitude of platforms from which we broadcast any opinion we like, we are made to feel that our view matters, that both ourselves and what we think are of paramount importance. On the one hand we are deeply suspicious of things like genetically modified food, nuclear energy and embryo research, without really understanding what they are or why we should feel that way, yet at the same time we are easily persuaded to make purchasing decisions by marketers' judicious use of scientific jargon that we have no hope of understanding. It is at this point, where hubris meets ignorance of ignorance, that there exists the perfect environment for those looking to manipulate and control us. After all, what could be better than a situation where those you are manipulating firmly believe that they are the ones who are in control?

Chapter 7
You Can Prove Anything With Facts

'You cannot reason people out of a position that they did not reason themselves into.' – *Ben Goldacre, author*

There is a hoary old chestnut beloved of supporters of the scientific method and it goes like this:

1. What star sign are you?
2. What blood group are you?

Most people get the first question right, but struggle to answer the second. Even if you're one of the few people who does know what blood group you are (well done, by the way) you can feel pleased that this makes you part of a pretty small minority. The implication is obvious: we know so little about the stuff that's coursing through our veins and yet we're all aware of something as trivial as our astrological star sign. Duh! Shame on us – we must be stupid.

In his book *Bad Science*, Ben Goldacre explores the reasons why clever people believe stupid things: 'When we reason informally – call it intuition if you like – we use rules of thumb which simplify the problems for the sake of efficiency.' He argues that these gut feelings are vulnerable to manipulation because we have no internal formula to determine what is true and what is false. When we get something wrong and the consequences are obvious, this is not a major problem because we learn quickly to adapt our behaviour. When the consequences are not so immediate or clear, however, correcting mistakes becomes much more difficult.

The result is that we can be fooled, or simply fool ourselves into thinking reality is other than it is. The question that concerns us in relation to Everything Now is not why this happens, but what happens as a consequence. We shall see that we rely upon our intuition to tell us not only what is right and wrong but, moreover, to decide what is important and unimportant.

People who are impressed and moved by the clarity and truth offered by rational arguments tend to believe that everyone else will respond to them in the same way. Unfortunately this is not the case. Anybody who has ever watched Professor Richard Dawkins argue on TV or YouTube, from a rational perspective, calmly, patiently and logically, that God can't possibly exist, will have noted how few of the inevitably less erudite Christians, Jews and Muslims he's up against ever congratulate him on the elegance of his argument.

As well as being credulous, human beings are emotional creatures. It is feeling not thinking that drives us: love and lust, kindness and greed, compassion and malice. Everybody wants to feel happy and nobody wants to be sad. It's true that we are also rational animals and that we all have the capacity to think logically when required, but those few people who are driven exclusively by reason, the rest of us tend to find quite boring. We might be respectful of Mr Spock's dedication to logical thought, and we may envy his ability to make decisions unfettered by any emotion, but we wouldn't really want to go for a night out with him.

It is easy to find examples of decisions where logic and reason play little, if any, role at all. Few of us brushed up on Immanuel Kant's *Critique of Pure Reason* before deciding with whom we would fall in love. There is no formula for deciding which music is good and which is bad, or which football team to support; what we eat is more a question of taste than one of health, and religious belief, much to Richard Dawkins' chagrin, is entirely a question of faith.

In a complex world, people tend to acquire only information that is useful or interesting to them. Let us return to the example of the star sign and blood group. Even if you don't believe in astrology it's very easy to work out what your star sign is. We all know our date of birth, and the twelve star signs roughly correspond to the months of the year. Not only are the star signs printed in the newspaper every day, but there are enough people who do believe in astrology for us to have been told on numerous occasions: 'Ah you're an Aries.' I do know what my star sign is, but I have no idea about the star sign of any of my friends, colleagues or family.

I do not know my blood group. There are two reasons for this. Firstly, finding out what blood group you are is much more challenging than knowing your star sign. It's not something you can test yourself and it's not something you can work out by looking for other signs. Nor is it printed in the newspaper every day. In fact, other than taking a blood test, there is no way of just picking up this knowledge – you can't work it out from your birthday. The second reason is because it doesn't matter. The only time knowing this information might become useful to me is if I was rushed into hospital requiring a transfusion and the doctors could not get hold of my medical records for some reason. Yet even in these unlikely circumstances, my wife, who is a doctor, assures me that they would never just take my word for it and so would give me a blood test anyway.

What we have is two pieces of information, which have no practical application to everyday life, but one is so easily discovered that you will know it, whether you want to or not, while the other requires the intervention of a specialist. One might be somewhat less frivolous than the other, but that is not the same as being more useful, nor is it reason enough to persuade us to search out the answer.

For some people – the ones who believe in astrology – knowing what star sign you are is important. There are plenty of them, so it would not be too difficult to find individuals with a deep understanding of the subject, who have dedicated years of study to horoscopy, many of whom may even be making a living out of it. The fact that they know so much about it doesn't make it true, but in certain circumstances – like when they are talking to other people who also believe in astrology, or trying to sell someone a horoscope – this knowledge that they have acquired definitely has a value. Indeed for the people who do believe in it, the 'facts' of astrology are no less real or true than the facts of evolution are to Richard Dawkins. It's just the process by which they have arrived at that truth that's different. Astrologers may argue passionately among themselves that Chinese horoscopy is better and more accurate than, say, that of the Ancient Greeks. They may feel that Russell Grant places too much emphasis on the waxing of Uranus, or even that Mystic Meg, with her popular predictions on the national lottery, was trivialising the discipline and giving it a bad name.

To rationalists like Dawkins, this kind of debate is akin to two bald men arguing over an imaginary comb. What Dawkins and his kin fail to understand is that imaginary combs are very good at brushing imaginary hair. Each person has a unique, personal interpretation of the world, constructed of discrete areas of ignorance and expertise, but, because we rely upon intuition, these areas do not necessarily correspond with truth and lies. Furthermore, the importance we place upon these interpretations is entirely subjective. The point is not whether or not the discussion about astrology is nonsense, but that to its followers a deep understanding can provide social currency that proves beneficial in terms of how they interact with their own version of the world.

Another example would be the knowledgeable football fan who relies upon their study and understanding of the game, not simply to enhance their enjoyment of the sport, but to provide social currency that can be used to help build and develop relationships with their friends and peers. Knowing about football is intrinsically of no more or less importance than knowing about astrology, but again, that's not to say it's of no value: socially, both have much more practical worth than knowing what your blood group is.

Another problem with relying on our intuition is that many truths are counter-intuitive; they just don't seem possible, or feel incorrect. When I was nine years old, my teacher told one particular story about a wise man who did a great service for the Emperor of China. As a reward the Emperor offered him the usual stuff – half the kingdom, the hand of his daughter or his weight in gold, something like that – but the man refused. Instead he produced a chessboard and said that all he wanted was for the Emperor to put a grain of rice on the first square and then double it for every square afterwards – putting two on the second square, four on the third and so on. The Emperor laughed at such a trifling request and granted the man his wish. But before his men had carried out that task for barely half the board, the man had already been given all of the rice in the city. It seemed unbelievable at the time that something so small could suddenly get so large. I had half a mind to try it out for myself with a draughts board when I got home, but my teacher went on to explain that there would be a million grains on the 21st square, and more than a trillion on the 41st square. There was not enough rice in the whole world, let alone China, to finish the final squares.

The story is an illustration of the mathematical principle of exponential growth and it demonstrates how very small things can suddenly become big things after a surprisingly small number of stages. The principle of exponential growth can be found in many areas from avalanches to economics, from the spread of contagious diseases to population growth.

Genealogy – the study of your family history – is a hobby that has gained in popularity over recent years. People indulge in it for many reasons – perhaps to get a sense of where one has come from, to provide a written history for future generations, but maybe simply to uncover interesting stories. People tend to trace their history through their father's side, probably because that's usually the one with the family name. However, you are literally only half your father, because half of your genes were inherited from your mother. This is equally true for everybody in the chain: your parents, your grandparents and your great-grandparents. So, as we go back through the generations, the number of people from whom you are directly descended will, just like the rice on the chessboard, increase exponentially. If we regard a generation as lasting 25 years, 21 generations would take us back to 1485, which means we are directly descended from around a million people alive at the time of the War of the Roses and the coronation of Henry VII. If we go back to the time of the Norman conquest in 1066, we are effectively descended from every living person in the old world – Asia, Africa and Europe.

These facts don't diminish the value of the hobby, nor am I suggesting that anyone endeavouring to put together a family tree is wasting their time.[1] What they do illustrate, however, is that it is not only convenient to ignore the facts, but in a world that is constructed on intuition, where the landscape is modelled by our own expertise and ignorance, it is also very easy to do so. And here we get to the heart of the matter. I can't imagine that anyone who indulges in genealogy will be persuaded to abandon the pastime as a result of reading the past few paragraphs, but even if I was to make the case more cogently, over the course of several books, articles and TV shows, I doubt anyone would be converted. For a kick-off, it would be very difficult to get them to engage with my idea (cutting through those 3,000 messages a day again) and most people would simply filter me out. Those that didn't would either construct counter-arguments or, where that failed, simply look for a poorly explained part of my thesis and try to use that weakness to discredit my entire proposition. Quite simply, if people are happy believing what they believe, and

[1] But it does mean that the next time somebody tells you about an interesting ancestor they've discovered, you can respond by revealing that you are a direct descendent of the Emperor Charlemagne, William the Conqueror and Genghis Khan.

they haven't used logic or reason to substantiate those beliefs, you aren't going to shift them.

In 2005, fast food restaurants came under a sustained attack for the damaging effects their products and up-selling policies (manifested in questions to customers like 'Do you want fries with that? Will that be a large fries?') were having on public health and particularly on increasing levels of obesity. Books like *Fast Food Nation* and *Fat Land* topped the bestseller lists, while the Morgan Spurlock film *Supersize Me* was a surprise box office hit. TV shows dedicated to healthier living started to appear – like *Fat Club* and the much-maligned *You Are What You Eat* – which performed well in the ratings. Although McDonald's always denied it was a response to this criticism, it was around this time that the company started to introduce healthier options onto the menu – like salads, wraps and fruit – and announced that its new menu would emphasise chicken and these new 'fresh foods' rather than hamburgers. This healthy options strategy proved to be a failure. The business performed badly and lost market share to its competitors. In response, the following year, McDonald's returned to its core proposition and put the burger back at the heart of its business. To celebrate the World Cup in Germany, it introduced a Big Mac that was 40 percent larger than the original and reintroduced the giant 'Big N' Tasty', a 460 kcal sandwich with almost half of that energy – 200 kcal – coming from fat. As a result a Big Mac meal with large fries and ketchup, including a large strawberry milkshake and Dairy Milk McFlurry, weighed in at a hearty 1,810 kcal. The result? An unhealthy profit.

I really don't think we needed the benefit of hindsight to explain what happened here. Quite simply, people who are concerned about eating healthily tend not to visit McDonald's, while those people who eat there a lot are probably not the ones reading *Fast Food Nation*. The views of these two groups are fixed: you can't change them, but we know that something must have been going on at McDonald's because sales were down, and went back up again after they refocused on the burger. After all, it's not as if people's behaviour doesn't change, we know that it does. This might seem like a contradiction, but it isn't. Understanding what happened at McDonald's is the key to understanding how Everything Now influences and persuades us to behave in certain ways.

Whatever side of the theological fence you're on, there is much to admire about Richard Dawkins' decision to take on organised religion. In *The God Delusion*, Dawkins employs the scientific method to demonstrate that a supernatural deity almost certainly does not exist and concludes that belief in such a deity is delusional. As an example of rationalist thought, the book is a tour de force. Focusing on the theist interpretation of God – that of an omnipotent, omniscient being who created the universe, is interested in human affairs and who should be worshipped – Dawkins explores all the main philosophical arguments in support of a creator, including Intelligent Design. He then employs the scientific method to challenge each one in turn and succeeds in proving that there is not one rational or logical reason to support belief in a deity.

Obviously, there were some people who found Professor Dawkins' conclusion a little contentious. If the atheist intellectual community was fulsome in its praise, then religious groups were united in their damning condemnation. Dawkins was criticised for not doing enough research into religion and for not having enough respect for the processes – like faith and doubt – by which people with religious convictions have come to the conclusion that God does exist.

Thanks to the Internet, the brouhaha surrounding *The God Delusion* is available for everyone to see. There are numerous interview clips on YouTube, where Dawkins, presumably on a global promotional tour to promote the book, is confronted by a procession of religious believers, all trotting out much the same arguments, sharing much the same level of disdain for his work.

Even if you don't like his perspicacity, you've got to respect the Prof's perseverance in the face of interviewers who are sometimes gauche, sometimes fatuous, sometimes even threatening, but most often, just downright rude. Dawkins responds to every question politely, patiently and respectfully, never losing his cool let alone his temper. Still, I couldn't help wondering at what point he began to feel that this tour of attrition really wasn't the way he wanted to be spending his retirement years.

If you watch one of the interviews on YouTube and take a look at the comments underneath, you'll find that all the atheist posters think Dawkins has won the arguments and performed well in the interviews – 'Brilliant logic, wonderfully explained. *The God Delusion* should be compulsive reading' – while all the religious posters feel that he's been made to look like the fool they always thought he was – 'Only an idiot would become atheist because there is no proof of the existence of God' – but what is striking about *The God Delusion* debate is that the two sides seem to be arguing about completely different things. In fact, at times, it's almost comical.

Religious people are unlikely to be swayed by rational arguments, because faith – really nothing more than a conceptualised version of intuition – is the foundation of their belief, not logic. And so it follows that their counter-arguments against Dawkins will be based upon faith and not reason. Faith is a complete anathema to Dawkins, a natural sceptic, who relies on an entirely evidence-based system to formulate his view of the world. For him it's always the best and only system, and for many people in the developed world it's almost always the best and only system; but there are also people who believe in God because they 'just do' or 'want to' or 'feel that they ought to' and they really require nothing more than that feeling to sway them.

In 2009, Fox News' Bill O'Reilly interviewed Dawkins. O'Reilly is a forthright, right-wing Christian commentator whose interviewing style makes Jeremy Paxman look conciliatory.

From the off, O'Reilly makes it obvious that he's not interested in hearing what Dawkins has to say: he's interested in showing him that he's wrong. Dawkins eruditely trots out what is, by now, the bog standard synopsis of his thesis. O'Reilly counters by saying he just doesn't believe that, because he doesn't; that he believes in God, because he does; and suggests that Dawkins is making just the same 'leap of faith' with his own belief in evolution. Dawkins, who let's remember has just written a book to demonstrate just how faithless he is, appears surprised if not staggered by this unconventional line of attack. He tries to explain that the entire point of the book (and, one imagines, this prolonged, and by now surely loathed, promotional tour) is that his belief in evolution doesn't require a leap of faith and all he is doing is simply providing evidence to support this belief and inviting people like O'Reilly, who believe in God, to do the same for theirs. Ignoring this completely, O'Reilly responds that he believes that Christ was the son of God, and while he can't prove that to be true, he does have faith, so for this reason alone has decided he's going to be 'throwing in with [Jesus]'. And so they continue, arguing in parallel from positions of reason and faith, apropos of nothing. Probably forever.

I would be amazed if anyone with strongly held spiritual beliefs who reads *The God Delusion* becomes an atheist as a consequence. There is no place for faith anywhere in the world view of Dawkins and his supporters, but likewise, if you've got faith, reason is only going to get in the way. Despite this failure, I do believe that the book was a great success: not just financially, but ideologically as well. I don't think that the point of *The God Delusion* was to convert the deeply religious. They will either just ignore the book completely or read it with the intention of finding a weak spot in the argument which they could use to discredit the whole, and I'm sure Richard Dawkins knows this as well. It's true that these are the kinds of people who were dragged onto TV to debate with him, ironically giving him a platform and allowing his ideas to reach a much wider audience than any of his previous books (the very things they'd ideally like to deny him) but these kinds of people were not the audience in themselves.

Similarly, while I've no doubt that Dawkins wants us to live in a Godless world, I don't think his core audience is the atheist intellectual movement either. True, his erudite book serves them well as a credo, and he himself will have inspired many to speak their mind for the first time or simply with more confidence, armed with potted versions of his own discourse. No, I believe the real success of Dawkins' book was not with the people sitting on either side of the fence, but with those sitting on it: the agnostic, the unsure and the uncertain.

The 19th-century German philosopher Georg Hegel gave the world the dialectic process, which posits that any idea, or thesis, must have an opposite – an antithesis. In this case the thesis 'God exists' attracts the antithesis 'God does not exist'. Hegel also believed the tension between the two would yield a new idea which combined them both – a synthesis: 'God might exist'. It is within this third group, the agnostic, where I believe Dawkins enjoyed most success. He may not have convinced every agnostic who read *The God Delusion* to become an atheist, but I suspect he did persuade an awful lot of them. Yet across the countless articles and TV and radio appearances, this group is all but invisible. Within all the oceans of media coverage, I can find scarcely a mention, yet surely the question of how successful he was or wasn't at influencing the undecided is the most important of all. And not only how successful *The God Delusion* was at persuading agnostics to become atheists, but whether it made them become less tolerant of religious intervention in secular life. The answers would be of interest and significance to everyone involved in the debate, regardless of whether they believe in a God or not.

Whatever the issue or the audience, it is within the agnostic group that behaviour can be most easily affected, which makes it even more remarkable that their voice is rarely heard and their views seldom taken into account, especially when one considers that anyone trying to change our behaviour – not just Richard Dawkins – will focus their efforts upon this group.

The outcomes of democratic elections are not determined by the party stalwarts – those who have read and digested the party manifestos, considered the issues and decided to put their X in the same place that they've always put it – but by the floating voter, the group that traditionally knows the least about politics, containing many people who don't make up their minds until the day of the election itself. They are they ones at whom all the posters, leaflets, advertising and personal appearances are aimed.

In the run-up to the 2010 election, Nick Clegg, a politician it's fair to say few people knew very much about at the time, saw his personal popularity, if not his party's, soar after a single good performance in the first ever live televised debate between the leaders of the three main political party's. His performance spurred the print media, generally sympathetic to either the Conservatives or Labour, to focus on some of his parties more controversial policies, and also resulted in a change in strategy by the two main parties, now beginning to take him seriously. It was only after a Herculean effort by all concerned that his support began to wane.

Marketers agree that it is almost impossible to change consumer behaviour by marketing activity alone. You can't stop people smoking simply by telling them it's bad for them, but if you make it difficult for them to smoke – for example, banning it in public places – you can have great success. Those who successfully change our behaviour are not the ones who challenge our ideas head-on, but the ones who push, nudge and persuade us to move in a new direction. Getting us to stop smoking is hard, but persuading us to consume low-tar cigarettes is easy, both appear to be taking us in the same direction – towards a healthier life – but one is a relatively easy change to make, the other, as I can testify, requires monumental willpower and effort.

The fact that the notion of a low-tar cigarette is entirely disingenuous is irrelevant. In the worldview of low-tar cigarette smokers, they want to believe that the decision they've taken is a positive step in the right direction. To them it's a question of faith rather than reason and, by simply applying a few selective facts to an area of voluntary ignorance, their behaviour can be directed. This is one of the ways that brands persuade us to try new products – products we never thought we needed. No one demanded low-tar cigarettes, but heightened awareness about the dangers of smoking succeeded in creating space into which that product could fit. 'I mean, logically, if tar is bad for me, less tar must be good for me? Mustn't it?'

Let us return to the example of McDonald's. The introduction of healthy options didn't turn on the people who never go to McDonald's, while the people who tuck into a Big Mac and fries regularly simply ignored them. All it did was to persuade the agnostics – the people who went there occasionally because they like a burger now and again and so don't feel the health risks apply to them – to eat at Burger King instead. For this group, the health concerns aren't an issue, because they might only go once a fortnight, so they simply filter them out. Perhaps McDonald's would have been more successful if it had introduced a low-fat burger instead.

It might not be important specifically to know what blood group you are, whether the Earth goes round the Sun, if dinosaurs and man co-existed or what season we're in, but our general ignorance of all these things and much more allows us to be exploited. And the extent of this exploitation is nothing short of amazing. We allow ourselves to be persuaded almost constantly that something is true, when we know that it cannot possibly be so.

Chapter 8
The 21 Signs of Ageing

'All Truths are easy to understand once they are discovered; the point is to discover them.' – *Galileo Galilei, philosopher, astronomer, mathematician*

We are living longer than ever before. Children born today can reasonably expect to see out the end of the century and the number of centenarians, already at a record high, is increasing at a rate that's guaranteed to give the Queen writer's cramp. 80 percent of the working population in 2010 will still be at work in 2020.

The birth rate is in decline and the average age of the population is increasing. Despite the fact that pensioners will soon outnumber those under 20, Everything Now is a young person's world. Once they reach middle age people tend to disappear from our TV and cinema screens – especially women – whilst old people are rarely seen, or heard, at all. Little wonder, then, that people want to stay looking as young as possible for as long as possible. Here again Everything Now is able to supply succour: not the secret of eternal youth itself, but the secret of feeling more youthful.

How do we beat the ageing process? Well, if you're going to fight something, you need to know what you're up against. Most of us have heard about the 'Seven Signs of Ageing' but far fewer know what they actually are. The answer seems to depend upon whom you ask. According to the customer service department at Procter and Gamble (P&G), the makers of Oil of Olay, the Seven Signs of Ageing are:

Lines and wrinkles
Rough skin texture
Dullness of skin's appearance
Larger appearance of pores
Blotchiness
Dry skin
Age spots

And not: [2]

Cerebral atrophy
Hypemetropia (long-sightedness)
Presbyacusis (deafness)
Osteoarthritis
Hypertension (high blood pressure)
Increased risk of myocardial infarction (heart attack) and stroke
Increased risk of falling and fractures

And definitely not: [3]

'Staying up' to watch *Question Time*
Forgetting where you've put your keys
Agreeing with something you've read in the *Daily Telegraph*
Listening to Radio 4
Mocking your children's taste in music
Not knowing which song is Number 1 in the 'Hit Parade'
Weighing two stone more than you used to

I make that 21 signs of ageing in all, but only seven can be found in the *Oxford Textbook of Medicine* and Oil of Olay can treat none of those. That's not to suggest that P&G is lying, far from it. Like

---

[2] *Oxford Textbook of Medicine*, Eds David A. Warrell, Timothy M. Cox and John D. Firth, Oxford: OUP, 2010
[3] By Steve McKevitt.

all cosmetics companies it simply chooses its words with great care. P&G does not claim that Oil of Olay can 'cure' *the* seven signs of ageing, only that it can 'fight' or 'treat' seven 'visible' signs of ageing.

P&G's list of the seven signs of ageing is subjective, not definitive. That doesn't mean that these are not seven signs of ageing, nor that Oil of Olay is not great at fighting or treating them, but it does mean that none of this has a basis in medicine. The company itself compiled the list, presumably in support of its marketing activity, a purpose it fulfils extremely well. In that sense, P&G's list has a lot more in common with Steve McKevitt's Seven Signs of Ageing™ than it does with those cited by the *Oxford Textbook of Medicine*. That is perhaps not the kind of ringing endorsement they are likely to plaster on the front of the box anytime soon, but I'm always open to offers.

Notice also that P&G claims only that its product can 'fight' or 'treat' seven signs of ageing, which is very different to saying that it can 'defeat' or 'reverse' them. I could for example 'fight' the British Parachute Regiment armed with just my fists, it's just highly unlikely that I will emerge victorious. Similarly a 'treatment' may do many things – alleviate suffering, extend life expectancy and quality, keep some symptoms in abeyance – without getting anywhere near a cure. Oil of Olay is a good-quality, if somewhat overpriced, skin moisturiser and everyone agrees that keeping your skin moisturised is a good thing, but it's not the elixir of eternal youth in a jar.

Anti-ageing products are big business, but the reality is that there is no miracle ingredient that is going to make you look ten years younger. In fact the most effective agents are nothing more than the now dreadfully unfashionable and boring vitamins A, C and E.

The most important factors in looking young for your age are all lifestyle. Around 30 percent of facial ageing is genetic, but the remaining 70 percent is down to repetitive sunlight, smoke, alcohol, diet and exercise. The message is simple: cut out the fags and the processed food, eat fresh fruit and vegetables, walk to work and drink more water. You'll start to look better. And better means younger.

I don't imagine for a second that these observations will come to you as some kind of earth-shattering enlightenment, but that really is the point. It might be very easy to prove that using Oil of Olay won't really stop the ageing process, but as Dawkins encountered during his World Book Tour of Attrition, there's an awful lot of people with enough faith to 'throw in with' the anti-ageing products regardless of whatever rational argument one chooses to produce. In 2010, the European market for facial skincare products, the beauty industry's strongest category, was worth $6.2 billion. Oil of Olay itself accounted for an estimated $2.8 billion of P&G's $79 billion turnover in 2009.

The people who use these products want to believe that they work. Just as moving to low-tar cigarettes is easier than giving up smoking, so using a face cream is less demanding, and more reassuringly expensive, than switching to a healthier lifestyle. Cutting down on the white wine and going for a run may be more effective, but it's also much more inconvenient. In fact, so eager are consumers to be convinced, they willingly accept all the hypoallergenic scientific-sounding jargon and Eastern mysticism that is often used to promote them without question. Indeed, they expect it. Cosmetics companies respond to this need by packing their marketing and advertising with just enough information to persuade us that product X is good for us. They don't lie – they don't have to – far from it: they only tell the truth. But sometimes they just don't tell us all of it.

The beauty-care sector is a mature market – Oil of Olay itself is over 60 years old – but while this, in theory, makes entry difficult, new products are being launched all the time. The recent trend has been for lines containing ingredients that, in addition to improving appearance, also claim to influence the biological performance of the skin itself. These so-called 'cosmeceuticals' are expensive, but usually positioned as a cheaper and safer alternative to cosmetic surgery and major non-surgical procedures, such as Botox injections. The marketing of these products is also changing.

In the past, glamorous models promoted anti-ageing products under the auspices that the brand in question was offering users the opportunity to attain similar levels of physical beauty. In Everything Now, there is less emphasis on achieving supermodel status; the focus is on seemingly more achievable, but actually more nebulous goals such as inner beauty and healthy lifestyles. This helps to make success much more difficult to measure, but just to reassure us, claims are now invariably backed by clinical trials and scientific evidence.

These products usually command premium prices, but the key is that they offer the user access to some kind of technological benefit that was previously denied to them 'Until Now!' for reasons that are never really explored. In 2006, P&G introduced an extension of the Olay brand called Regenerist: a collagen-based anti-ageing cream. The efficacy of smearing collagen on your face in order to halt the ageing process is moot, but the campaign P&G used to launch it demonstrates a remarkable understanding not just of the desire of the Everything Now audience to be shown how to think in a certain way, but of our willingness to buy into a fiction if we feel that doing so will help us to get what we want. It also highlights some of the techniques that can be employed by brands to achieve this.

Nadine Baggott, a handsome, blonde woman who looks to be in her early forties, is something called a 'celebrity beauty editor' and she tells me that, in her job, she gets to learn lots of celebrity beauty secrets. I know this because she is the star of the advert I'm watching as I write, which was created to launch Olay Regenerist. Now Nadine doesn't just learn beauty secrets from celebrities – oh no – she also relies on the information she gets from 'beauty skincare experts' to discover a few beauty secrets of her own.

To underline this fact, we now see a shot of Nadine doing just that. We can't hear what the skin care experts are saying, but they are in white lab coats, one of them is wearing glasses and Nadine is taking notes, just like a proper journalist, so it must be something really important. Blimey, it is! And Nadine's going to tell us about it right now. You see, Nadine thinks the hottest anti-ageing ingredients around are – better get a pen – Pentapeptides KTTKS. 'What in heaven's name are they?' I wonder. Hang on a minute – what luck! Up there on the screen are the very beauty secret notes that Nadine was taking earlier on. I can see that they are tiny pieces of protein molecules that can actually help to renew the skin's surface. That's amazing! Who'd have thought that wiping the years away could be so easy?

Alas, Nadine hints there might be a catch. Remember she said these were celebrity beauty secrets? Well you'd probably expect to pay celebrity prices to get your hands on these high-tech, anti-ageing ingredients wouldn't you? I know I would… But wait! This is Everything Now, remember. Nadine tells us she has 'discovered' that Pentapeptides KTTKS are available in Olay Regenerist, a moisturiser that only costs around £20. And that, as she says, is hardly a celebrity price, is it? I'm no Marxist, but I have to say that Nadine's suggestion that the famous should be made to pay more for things than ordinary people strikes me as quite radical. But then this comes from someone who, by her own admission, has been stealing beauty secrets from celebrities in order that we, the poor, can have them as well. Nadine's nothing less than a better-looking, modern-day Robin Hood.

Before she leaves, Nadine makes it clear that she recommends Olay Regenerist because it makes her skin smoother and fuller as well as looking like new skin. Now that, she concludes, is a beauty secret worth knowing.

This advert was the centrepiece of a multi-million pound advertising campaign and consequently shown countless times on primetime television. Yet the inference is that Nadine has stumbled across such a huge celebrity beauty secret that she felt a civic obligation to let us all know about it. One can only speculate how she raised the finance necessary to facilitate this.

To engage with this advert, on any level, requires a monumental suspension of disbelief. Of course, everybody watching knows that the only reason Nadine really says any of these things is because she is paid to do so by Procter and Gamble. But if you are one of those people who has 'thrown in with' the anti-ageing products then it makes perfect sense that you should also want to subscribe to Nadine's farrago of fact and fiction. Certainly Regenerist has gone on to become one of the leading anti-ageing products on the market.

Beauty products may not feature anywhere in Maslow's Hierarchy of Needs and ultimately using a face cream won't cause anyone any harm, but there are less flippant examples where exactly the same processes are at work, which have far more significant implications for us all.

A constant supply of electricity is something we take completely for granted. Without it modern life as we know it would collapse. We use it to heat and light our homes and cities; it powers everything from factories to the Internet. Without electricity there would be no food on the table, no clean water in the taps and no fuel in our cars. Yet ask most people how electricity works and they won't be able to give you an answer.

Electricity is a curious thing. It instinctively feels familiar; something we use all the time, yet it is also something of a mystery. We can't see it, smell it or taste it and those rare occasions when we can feel it are almost always unpleasant. While humans have known about electricity for thousands of years – the Ancient Greeks were aware of static and it fascinated Pythagoras (he of the theorem) who wrote about it extensively – but it is only in the last 150 years that we've worked out how to do something useful with it.

Here's how it works. The movement of electrons causes electricity, tiny negatively charged particles that surround every atom. In some circumstances the electrons can be made to flow from atom to atom in metals. Electricity is produced at a power station. Fuel is used to boil water; when the water boils, the high-pressure steam produced is used to drive turbines, which in turn generate electricity. These generators are nothing more than enormous magnets that spin inside coils of metal wire. Electricity and magnetism are related physical forces, and it's the movement of the magnets that causes the electrons to flow in the wires. The flow of these electrons is called electric current and this current likes to travel back to where it came from, this is called a 'circuit'. The power lines extend out from a power station and into our homes and offices through the positive hole in a plug socket, pass through our appliances, and out of our homes via the negative hole in the socket, eventually leading all the way back to the power station, where the process is repeated again.

The volume of electricity flowing through power lines is much greater than any of us need, so transformers are used to distribute energy to each household. Transformers drain off a percentage of the energy carried in the power line and transmit it to smaller circuits, like those in an office or house. In each building there are a number of circuits each allowing for different amounts of power. Finally when you plug in an appliance, the electricity can be used to create light or heat or even sound. It can even run motors that will keep things cold.

This National Grid, into which we are all connected, is itself a recent innovation, only coming into being in 1949 as a result of the Electricity Act of 1947, which nationalised the utility. It might seem strange to us now, given how much we've come to rely upon it, but at the time there was a great deal of organised opposition to achieving a national supply of electricity. The population was far less urbanised than it is today, and many people living outside towns and cities objected to the unsightly pylons ruining the landscape. There were also concerns about the potential risks to public health that high-voltage electric cables criss-crossing the countryside might cause. People questioned whether there would ever be enough demand for electricity: after all we'd survived for hundreds of years without it and most people were perfectly happy with coal, oil and gas to provide them with heat and light. In fact the opposition was so fierce that the government embarked on a major public information initiative, advertising the benefits of this new, clean source of energy and giving people ideas for what they could do with it.

Knowing or not knowing how electricity works is one of those things that doesn't have any impact on how we live our lives day to day, and in that respect it can be regarded as no more nor less important or useful than knowing how many planets there are or the names of the moons of Saturn. But we are moving into a future that will require us to rely less and less upon burning fossil fuels – whether for reasons of climate change or simply because there is not an inexhaustible supply. The means by which oil, gas and coal are to be replaced and how our electricity is then supplied are therefore of paramount importance.

Unfortunately, there is not one single obvious solution to this problem and, among the policymakers and politicians of various flavours, there is no consensus regarding the best way forwards. In their respective 2010 manifestos, the Conservatives said they wanted to establish at least two Marine Energy Parks, speed up the planning process for new nuclear power plants and only permit coal-fired power stations with clean carbon technology to be built. The Labour Party also wanted to build new nuclear power stations, but was much more committed to renewable energy, promising £1 billion private funds, with £1billion public funding, to create a 'Green Bank' to drive investment in it. Meanwhile, the LibDems didn't have a place for nuclear power at all, believing that wind power offers the best long-term solution and committing £400 million to a scheme that would repurpose shipyards to make turbines.

What all this means is that, ultimately, the democratic process will determine how the UK's energy is supplied in future. In other words, it is us who will decide which route to go down. Now, we have learned that very few of us are expert enough to be able to make an informed decision, but we also know that people don't really need to be conversant with all the facts before they start to have strong opinions. The obvious solution would appear to be 'provide people with more information', but if we do that, something interesting, unexpected and not entirely helpful happens.

Take the issue of whether we should build more nuclear power stations or not. We can all agree that it's one solution to the energy problem, but opinion is vehemently divided as to whether it's the right solution. To help us make our own minds up, we could sift through the massive body of primary source material, but the science is complicated and this would be an onerous undertaking for anyone without a background in academic research. A less daunting option might be to refer to secondary sources; reports and news stories written by experts who have already read, digested and interpreted the primary material, who can offer an explanation in terms we ordinary people can understand. The caveat to this is that these sources are unlikely to be entirely neutral and will contain the commentators' own analysis of the facts.

Consider also that people tend to get very antsy when you use words like 'nuclear energy' and 'radioactive' – especially those between the ages of 40 and 65, who will have spent their formative years with the Cold War threat of nuclear holocaust permanently hanging over them. Nuclear power has the weight of seven decades of almost entirely negative publicity bearing down on its shoulders. From the appalling scenes of carnage that accompanied the bombings of Nagasaki and Hiroshima, through the explosion of the reactor at Chernobyl, to the post-tsunami meltdown at the Fukushima reactor in Japan; from powerful fictional accounts of the world post-apocalypse of *On the Beach*, *The War Game*, *The Day After* and *Threads*, through power-plant-based dramas like *Silkwood* and *The China Syndrome* to the sensationalist 'super-mutant' fantasies of popular video games, films and comic books: the vocabulary of nuclear war is almost cosily familiar. Words and phrases such as 'meltdown', 'duck and cover', 'nuclear winter', 'fallout', 'megaton', 'dirty bomb' and 'mutually assured destruction' are used and understood widely. We all know what happens when nuclear power goes wrong and how dire the consequences are for all of us. Or at least we think we do.

Radiation in high doses is deadly, but there is evidence to suggest that we overestimate the dangers of radioactivity at lower levels. Much of our early thinking is based on what happened after the bombings in Japan, where victims were subjected to massive doses of radiation. Studies of the fauna and flora around Chernobyl, where background radiation levels are still considered dangerously high, have revealed that it shows little sign of being adversely affected. Indeed the biggest change that has occurred, the continued absence of mankind, has been entirely positive from the perspective of animals and plants.

Post-9/11, a great deal of coverage was dedicated to the threat posed to cities in the West by a terrorist-detonated dirty bomb. A dirty bomb, not to be confused with an atomic or nuclear bomb, is a conventional explosive device that contains radioactive material – say waste from a nuclear power plant. Such a device would cause little physical damage, but as it explodes the radioactive material it contained could be dispersed over an area of several miles. Most reports in the mainstream media suggested that this would render affected areas uninhabitable for up to 20 years. This view gained popularity when the BBC broadcast a 2003 documentary called *Dirty Bomb* as part of its flagship science series *Horizon* and followed it up with a primetime drama the following year called *Dirty War*, which purported to show what would happen if a dirty bomb was detonated in the City of London.

Despite all the hype, a dirty bomb is not much more dangerous than a conventional device. Ironically, almost all the additional danger is as a result of the psychological impact the explosion would have on us – due to the media-generated hysteria, misreporting and misinformation – rather than any radioactive material it may contain. The US Department of Energy carried out a test explosion of a dirty bomb in 2004 and concluded that, even if nothing was done, background radiation levels would return to normal in just

12 months. Assuming all residents stayed where they were, levels of radiation would be 'fairly high', but not high enough to cause serious illness or death. The analysis of the Chernobyl disaster supported this view, where the impact of the reactor explosion on people living in the surrounding region has proved to be negligible (those in the immediate vicinity were evacuated).

So here we have a complex subject, where a great deal of information is available, but much of it is conflicting or tainted by the personal opinions of the commentator, and where there is little consensus even among the experts, let alone the political parties. Returning to our original question, one would imagine that in these circumstances it's impossible for a layperson to form a view about whether building more nuclear power stations is a good idea. In fact, the opposite is true: it's an issue about which almost everyone you meet will have an opinion, and one that's very likely to be strongly held.

The environment is a perennial subject of phone-in debates and online discussions. Watch or listen to any of the myriad channels of communication allowing ordinary citizens to 'have their say' and you'll quickly come to realise that, while members of the public are clear in terms of what they think, very few of them are conversant with the science, and consequently are less clear about why they think that way. People do not usually approach these contentious subjects with an open mind. What happens instead is that they start with a view – in this instance whether they think nuclear power stations are a good or a bad idea – and then look for information that supports that view and filter out information that doesn't. Whatever they think, they will almost certainly find there is a lot of information to support it, and persuasive arguments that they can appropriate for their own purposes.

Again, 'So what?' you might say. 'If it's so complicated, let's leave it up to the politicians to decide.' The issue here is that politicians are in the business of winning elections, which happen every four or five years. Consequently they are very sensitive to what the public thinks, but whether that thinking was based on the latest scientific research or the latest *Sunday Times* column by Rod Liddle is immaterial to them. Spending huge amounts of money on something that is very unpopular today, but which will deliver a benefit some 20 or 30 years down the line, is never going to be a vote winner.

In 2006, I was invited to participate in a closed meeting with several political leaders of UK cities. At the time the UK was in the midst of its biggest building boom for 50 years. The discussion was about 'me-too' architecture and the danger that city centres were losing their individuality and identity, with any one beginning to look much like any other. I suggested that one solution might be that council planning committees should be encouraged to take more risks in terms of the designs and schemes that they approved. I was cut short by the council leader of one of the biggest cities in the UK, who told me, to a chorus of approval, that what I didn't understand was: 'You can't have radical design when you've got annual elections. You'd never stay in office!' I really felt there was no answer to that.

Only one thing is certain, whenever the location for a nuclear power station is announced there is always a furore. Whether we will be any closer to determining how we stop an energy problem from turning into an energy crisis as a result is far less certain.

Nor is this a problem peculiar to nuclear energy. If you don't like the idea of wind turbines blotting your view across the valley, simply look for articles and research questioning or criticising their efficiency and you will find them. There's no need to stop there. At the time of writing if you conduct a Google search for the phrase 'smoking does not cause cancer' (including the inverted commas) you will find 54,000 pages dedicated to the topic. Some of the arguments are well reasoned and well written, others appear to be rants of the borderline insane, while some, like this blog post, are simply pedantic:

> The FACT of the matter is: SMOKING DOES
> NOT CAUSE CANCER! Smoking may, in some
> cases, improve the ability of the actual cause of
> cancer to take hold. But, it DOES NOT CAUSE
> CANCER. There is a huge difference there.

I can appreciate that if you're an immortal twenty-something with your whole life ahead of you, then this 'fact' could offer a slice of psychological comfort as you're ploughing through today's second pack of Marlboro Lights. It's easy to remember and repeat and gives people the impression that you might know what you're talking about. But believe me, when you're a fifty-something gasping for air on a Oncological Ward as small cell metastases rampage though what's left of your body, whether your cancer was caused by cigarettes or whether smoking 'improved the ability of the cancer to take hold' will really make no difference to you at all.

Even the attitude of researchers themselves may lead to subtle differences in the way they conduct experiments or analyse the data. This is not to imply fraud, but it is true that believers do tend to produce positive results, while sceptics carrying out the same experiment will tend to find nothing. I do often wonder whether Jeremy Clarkson's vitriolic opposition to the environmentalist lobby is born out of a genuine belief that the CO_2 exhaust emissions are not responsible for climate change, or merely a genuine desire that they are not.

Everything Now has given us access to more information than ever before, and resulted in us receiving more information than ever before, but it has not made us wiser and it certainly hasn't improved the quality of our decisions. It has, however, made it much easier for us to reinforce our prejudices. This does not mean we can't be influenced – on the contrary, our ideas and opinions are subjected to more manipulation than ever before – it's just that the means of persuasion have become more insidious.

Part 3: Mind Control

Mind *noun*

The element of a person that enables them to be aware of the world and their experiences, to think, and to feel; the faculty of consciousness and thought.

1. A person's ability to think and reason.
2. A person's memory.
3. A person's attention.

Control *noun*

The power to influence or direct people's behaviour or the course of events.

1. The restriction of an activity, tendency, or phenomenon.
2. (*verb with object*) To determine the behaviour or supervise the running of.
3. (*verb with object*) To maintain influence or authority over.

Chapter 9
Making Your Mind Up

'Public opinion is a permeating influence, and it exacts obedience to itself; it requires us to drink other men's thoughts, to speak other men's words, to follow other men's habits.' – *Walter Bagehot, 19th-century political essayist*

Most of us will be lucky enough to have a close friend. Someone who we can trust and rely upon, sharing secrets and confidences; someone to whom we can turn in times of adversity. Similarly, most of us will be able to rattle off the name of at least one celebrity we cannot stand. Maybe a cocky presenter, goofy comic or an earnest thespian; perhaps an anodyne musician or some moody sportsperson. Our opinion of both the friend and the personality may well be held with equal conviction, but the kind of information we use to make each judgement is very different in nature.

We form all opinions on the basis of experiences and information, but this data is drawn from two entirely different views of the world. The first is our personal worldview, which is compiled almost exclusively from information we take in through the senses in the form of experiences. These experiences can come from many different sources – interactions with people around us, conversation or personal contact, things that happened at work, social events, holidays and so on. Sensory information is intense, memorable and it accumulates over time. It is these experiences that are primarily responsible for building up our own unique areas of expertise and ignorance and they determine the way we will behave in the future. Those experiences that engage or entertain us, we will seek to repeat; those that cause us to respond negatively, we will attempt to avoid.

Just because our personal worldview is the result of these first-hand, intense experiences does not mean it is entirely rational; our emotions also play a huge part. For example, you may have decided that you hate Belgium simply because, on the way back from a school trip, you once spent 48, rain-swept hours at Oostende Ferry Terminal where you had a bag stolen, containing all your presents and clothes. If it was my job to change your mind, I am unlikely to achieve success by simply telling you that you're mistaken and explaining how good Belgium really is.

The best chance I have of succeeding is if I can give you an equally intense, positive experience to displace the original. For example, I could find out what your favourite things are – and for the purposes of this example, let's say they are beer with fruit in it; detective stories featuring kids, dogs and sea captains; and small, well-preserved medieval cities – and then give you a first-hand experience of what Belgium has to offer in respect of those: a weekend in Bruges, a copy of *Tintin in Tibet* and four pints of Boon Framboise. It is important to remember, though, that even this kind of bold gambit is not guaranteed to change your opinion.

The second view of the world is our broad worldview, which consists of everything that is outside of our personal experience. We develop this view not by using our senses, but vicariously, relying exclusively on information that has already been interpreted by at least one other person. This could be through interaction with family, friends, peers, teachers and colleagues, or it could be the books or magazine articles we read, the websites we browse, or the TV shows and movies we watch. Our favourite way of receiving this information is in the form of stories. Everybody likes stories, not only are they engaging and entertaining, but they are also much easier to remember than raw data or information. Many people will know who Alfred the Great is, and of those, many will be able to recall that he is famous for burning some cakes, but few will be able to recall the dates of his birth, accession, or death. None of these 'facts' has any practical value, but one is easy to remember, because it is so unusual: what other monarch is synonymous with overcooked puddings? Dates, on the other hand, are much more difficult to recollect. Can you, for example, recall what date it was five Tuesdays ago?

In forming our broad worldview, these vicarious sources act like a sixth sense, providing us with the raw information to form opinions about issues, people or products for which we have no first-hand experience. This opinion is further shaped and influenced through further investigation via social interaction, or some form of media.

The downside of relying on vicarious information to form a view is that we are only ever provided with a précis (and often a précis of a précis) rather than the whole picture. And moreover, a précis that we can never be certain is based on an entirely trustworthy source in the first place. Often, though, this is more than enough for us. A decent review may be all it takes to persuade us to go and see the new Harry Potter film, or to decide that we can't live without a smartphone. A good rating on TripAdvisor may reassure us that our hotel booking won't be a disappointment. And if you've no bad opinion of Belgium, my romantic and hilarious anecdote about a family canoeing trip through the Ardennes during a thunderstorm may tempt you into taking a summer vacation at Durbuy, the enchanting and self-proclaimed smallest city in the world.

Making this kind of judgement becomes habitual, so we can make them even when the amount of information is tiny and the quality dubious. Often these judgements are harmless. No one is going to suffer particularly if you decide on the basis of a poor review that you're not going to like the new Madonna album, but deciding that you don't like Romanians because you read a negative article about them on the Internet, or because you once heard someone proclaim that 'they are lazy' can cause all sorts of problems.

Compared with the richness that shapes our personal worldview, our broad worldview is two-dimensional. We can place almost anything into one of just three categories: things we like, things we don't like and things about which we are ambivalent. Contrast this with your personal worldview. If you think about your circle of friends or acquaintances, then unless you're a member of some religious cult, I'm guessing it's fair to say that none of them is perfect. They will have a mix of qualities, some good and some bad, but given that they are your friends, you've probably decided the former outweigh the latter to varying extents. So, Barry might be a very funny guy, and great company, but also completely unreliable. Ian, on the other hand, is solid and dependable, but tends to talk about golf a bit too much. Sarah is a great mum and very helpful, but can be a bit of a control freak. Hannah is very warm and gregarious, but terrible at staying in touch.

For this reason, conflicts with work colleagues, family or friends can often be quite difficult to resolve. There's a saying that there are three versions of every story: yours, mine and the truth. In most situations there is never one person entirely at fault and synthesising the truth from two different versions of the same story is no walk in the park. Relationships often break down for complicated reasons, so complicated, in fact, that many people resort to counselling from an impartial third party to help them arrive at a resolution. We also know that a person's situation can determine their behaviour: the most gregarious, happy-go-lucky of people can become sullen and moody if they're tired or under pressure at work. And we all make mistakes. We put our foot in it, say inappropriate things, misjudge situations, and occasionally do things that we might regret. When we feel wronged, sometimes we forgive, kiss and make up then move on, but other times we don't and we hold a grudge, and occasionally we might simply act as if nothing has happened. In short, through our experiences, we understand that our lives and relationships are complex, that people are multifaceted not just 'goodies and baddies'. As a result our personal worldview is exactly that: unique to ourselves. Mine is different to yours and, in turn, to everyone else's. It is not something that can easily or helpfully be distilled down into component parts.

It is rare that we use any of this knowledge to inform our broad worldview. In contrast to those opinions formed in our personal worldview, our stance on world events, current affairs, public figures, celebrities, foreign countries and the like is often stereotypical: we are either for or against people, ideas and places; products are either good or bad; events make us either happy or sad. We don't like him, she's a saint, he's a crook, it would be a disaster for the country, they can't be trusted, he's a junkie, she's a liar, they're pathetic, she's a winner, he's a loser, it's rubbish, it's brilliant. The strength of this opinion is often in inverse proportion to the amount of information upon which it is based. A single gobbet of information can be all it takes to provoke the most violent of responses.

In October 2009, Philip Laing, a 19-year-old student from Macclesfield, was photographed relieving himself against a war memorial in Sheffield city centre after a night of heavy drinking. The following day the *Daily Mail* published the picture on its website and, almost instantly, Laing became the most hated man in Britain. His subsequent arrest was celebrated as a victory for common decency. During his trial, District Judge Anthony Browne didn't mince his words. He let Laing know just how heinous his crime was and what kind of retribution the legal system would take: 'The image of you urinating over the poppy wreath on the war memorial in this city will make most people turn away in disgust, shock and sadness.' He added that all sentencing options were open, including custody.

What can we learn from this? Well first of all, let's look at the incident itself. A reprehensible and disrespectful act, to be sure, certainly deserving some form of chastisement, but prison? Who could pretend that this was a unique example of irresponsible or reckless behaviour by a drunken undergraduate? Why did we need to make an example of him? Is urinating on war memorials spiralling out of control? Is this an activity from which young people need to be deterred? Many of us got really drunk when we were in our late teens and did something we regretted afterwards, but we didn't have those indiscretions broadcast to the world. The judge was right in one respect: what caused most offence was the image. The image that the *Daily Mail* chose to publish, because it knew it would cause offence. Would the world be any the worse had the paper chosen not to do so? Was this really in the public interest?

But this was no flash in the pan. The story of the urinating student didn't go away and the *Mail* ran with it for almost a month. Following the initial report, the paper interviewed the 'Grandson of a World War I Veteran'. Well, there can only be a few million of them in the country, so why not get one single person to speak on behalf of them all? He was, unsurprisingly, 'angry and disgusted'. Next, the paper published an article drawing a comparison between, 'Two very different Britons: The student who defiled a war memorial and the soldier who died at Passchendaele'. The piece concluded that sports technology student Laing had it much easier than his 1917 counterpart Edwin Levers, who was mown down by German machine-gunners. The same day the paper also ran a story about another veteran, Matthew Weston, who had lost both legs whilst on a tour of duty in Afghanistan. In this article Weston pondered, 'Even while I was fighting I was paying my taxes to fund wasters like him [Laing].'

The next day the readers were treated to a story about nightclub bouncers who were 'stand[ing] guard at a WWI memorial urinated on by a drunken student'. They had volunteered themselves for this noble and courageous service, in response to the 'national outcry' caused by the image. Just to make sure you knew what caused the outrage, the offending picture was printed again. And again. And again.

Laing quit university on 15 December, the day before a college disciplinary hearing was due to convene. It was less than six weeks since the story had broken; a period of relentless media coverage during which the *Daily Mail* had printed the picture of Laing's indiscretion on no less than nine separate occasions. How much happier must John Levers, the late Edwin Levers, Matthew Weston, the unnamed bouncers and all the *Daily Mail*'s outraged staff and readers have been, at the prospect of never again having to look at such an offensive image? Well, at least until the following year, when the whole sorry business was dredged up again during the 2010 freshers' season.

One picture is all it took for many people to make up their minds about Philip Laing. I don't know whether – in real life – Philip Laing is a latter-day saint who made a terrible mistake or a despicable cad who deserved everything that happened to him (although I would be willing to bet that, like most of us, he's somewhere between the two), but then neither does the *Daily Mail* or its readers. The Philip Laing in this story is not real. He is an artefact: the epitome of a feckless, drunken, student layabout, with too much money, too little responsibility and zero respect for his elders and betters. His image became a totem for everybody who holds these prejudices: 'Look at the youth of today. Look how awfully they behave. Don't you just hate them?'

The *Daily Mail* online thoughtfully provided people holding this view with a platform from which they could have their say, which naturally they did. A selection of the comments posted are presented here verbatim. They do nothing to improve anyone's understanding, simply serving to reinforce the stereotype further:

'As someone who's grandfather died in WWI and Dad fought in WWII, all I can say is this guy (sorry, can't call him a "man") is a PIG! He isn't worthy of even "weeing" on the memorial. What an absolute disgusting show of disrespect. He should be ashamed of himself and his parents should be ashamed for raising such a disrespectful person.' Kerry, Livermore CA, USA.

'shameful. he should be made to join the army.. go front line.. get shot at and then see what BIG man he is.. a complete waste of a human being in my opinion!' Tina Ingamells, Brunei.

'It sickens me that someone would actually do that to the war memorial when so many people gave there lifes for our country for a cause and still are.' Paul Todd, Southampton.

Stories like this leave no mark on the world. There is no legacy, no insight, no new understanding: society categorically does not change; yet they achieve enormous levels of coverage and notoriety. Who knows what became of Philip Laing, but for a few weeks, the *Daily Mail* was interested in every area of his life and told its readers that they were too. Reporters trawled his Facebook postings for titbits of information, contacted family and 'friends' for a reaction or salacious quote and even speculated whether he would wear a poppy at his November trial (How dare he!) and whether he wouldn't (How dare he!). No doubt whoever was advising Laing at the time will have told him that things may be bad now, but in time it would all blow over. And they'd be right, because all Philip Laing was to the *Daily Mail* was a source of content. And once he ceased to be a source of content, so they ceased to be interested in him.

It is not the type of story that has changed – since the 1960s, the British tabloid press especially has loved to shock, appall and titillate its readers in equal measure – but the timing. Papers used to contain yesterday's news. Unable to cover events as they happened, they covered ones that had already happened. The rolling TV and radio news networks and innumerable online news channels, blogs and emails, put paid to this. These outlets have an enormous, insatiable appetite for news which means that demand for content – which must be delivered instantly – has never been greater. Unfortunately, despite this increase in demand, the supply of news remains much the same as it ever was. Thus, what was once delivered comfortably in two 30-minute bulletins each day, must now be spread across 24 hours, 7 days a week.

In response to this challenge, three things have happened. First of all, unable to talk about the past, newspapers have started gazing into the future and telling us about events before they have happened: 'The Prime Minister will announce later today…', 'Schools will be told…', 'Train fares expected to rise…', 'A company statement is anticipated…'.

Secondly, there has been a huge increase in the amount of analysis – the media's equivalent of a bulking agent – which provides scope for much more 'content' to be wrung out of an individual story. Where stories were once simply reported – 'A dog was run over. The tragedy was blamed on careless driving' – they are now also discussed forensically, explored from every possible angle, with a view to extrapolating further topics for discussion. Using our canine tragedy as an example, one could reasonably expect to hear the views of the owner, the driver, the views of other dog owners and drivers; a road safety group representative to talk about the broader picture; an animal welfare group representative to talk about a different broader picture; and an animal psychologist to speculate why the dog decided to cross the road in the first place, which would all in turn lead to a discussion about the macro issues of dogs getting run over, why Britain has the worst survival rates in Europe and why the government isn't doing more to stop it. Finally, one of the regular columnists would tell us what they think the story really means and give us a helpline number that we can call if we've suffered any similar experiences to those highlighted by the story.

Finally, and most importantly, swathes of editorial space, both on the page and on air, is dedicated to what is known as User Generated Content; that is, items and articles created not by journalists but by the readers, viewers and listeners.

In the past, media outlets – newspapers, magazines, TV channels and radio stations – were fairly straightforward businesses to run.

Usually, there were only one or two revenue streams: advertising and, in the case of printed media, copy sales. If you know how much advertising space you have available to sell and how much you can charge for it, it's fairly easy to work out what your turnover is going to be. From there you can then determine how much cost you can bear and how much profit you'll stand to make. What's more, there are only two factors that affect how much you can charge for advertising: how big your audience is and what kind of people they are.

During the original dotcom boom, many new media businesses were launched – Ananova, Sportal, Soccernet, Sportinglife.com, Rivals.net, icrunch to name just a few – using exactly the same model. Most of them didn't last long, because with no money from content sales, there just wasn't enough advertising to go round. More than ten years later, with advertising budgets in steady decline, it's surprising just how many online businesses still cling on to this business model, but this only serves to show just how challenging it is to turn content into money.

Today, the business models of media organisations are anything but straightforward. What was once called Third-Line Revenue or VAS (Value Added Sales), which is the supplementary income from everything other than ads or copy sales, has now become core business. Whether it's sponsorship, events, online stores selling books, downloads, insurance and travel, paid-for 'advertorials' and supplements or even gambling, media businesses will take money from as many sources as they can.

This has affected definitions of what is newsworthy, which have been pushed way beyond what might previously have been regarded as in the public interest. Commerce has permeated editorial coverage, blurring the line between advertising and editorial. The best exponents of this are the broadsheet Sunday papers. An average issue of *The Observer*, *Sunday Times* or *Sunday Telegraph* contains around 500,000 words, with the *Mail on Sunday* not far behind. To read an entire issue from cover to cover – having spent less to buy your paper than you did on the cup of coffee to go with it – would take around 36 hours. And by completing this task, you will have absorbed more information than the average 18th-century British citizen encountered in a lifetime. Almost all of the articles contained in the paper itself, and everything you read in the supplements, will have been trying to sell you something. Books, cars, property, holidays, Sky Sports subscriptions, concert and theatre tickets, restaurants, food, insurance, video games, movies, music, fashion, furniture, political parties, universities, independent schools… you name it.

Even the articles that look like news are probably hawking something covertly. PR is the invisible source of this information and it makes up the majority of things you see and hear in the news. PR is big business. The sector is worth £6.5 billion per year in the UK alone and all this money is being spent in order to shape the way you think about everything from Pepsi Cola, the new Renault Clio and Katie Price, to global warming and the Labour Party. The weight of this activity bears down on the print, online and broadcast journalists.

Many publications are entirely PR driven. *Hello* and *OK* are the most famous examples, but there are hundreds of others. There are things you can look out for to identify PR from real stories – for example, the absence of any conflict or jeopardy, which are usually key news ingredients, is a dead giveaway. 'Good company does quite well' is never going to generate headlines, so any story that presents an individual or organisation in a positive light – about a survey it's commissioned perhaps – is probably PR as well. Within publications that rely on public relations heavily, but not exclusively, PR and news will be virtually indistinguishable to the untrained eye, but once you know what to look for it's easy to spot the story and the source.

Newspapers may have begun the trend of bulking out their pages with celebrity news, gossip and columnists, but the other news channels have been quick to follow. Even *Question Time*, the BBC's old political-debating warhorse, has been jazzed up by the inclusion of pop stars, actors, novelists, comedians and other celebrities on the panel. The backside of a personality with a hobbyhorse to ride or a drum to bang can command just as much on-screen sofa-space as one with a film, book or album to flog. If Chris Martin, lead singer with Coldplay, thinks that world poverty is wrong and that something should be done about it – like wearing a coloured wristband with 'End Poverty Now!' written on it – his publicist will be able to line up, in a matter of hours, a raft of TV, radio and print interviews that he can use to get his point across. And if Chris fancies writing a few articles himself, then a guest column in one or more of the broadsheets will be easily gleaned. This happens all the time. The quality of Chris's wristband idea is irrelevant: like Philip Laing he is merely a source of content; content that will appeal to readers, viewers, browsers and listeners and encourage them in turn to 'have their say' and ring in, write in or post their comments, providing yet more analysis and yet more content.

Let's not be too hard on the media, just like the universities with their fatuous degrees, it is only responding to our demand for Everything Now and, similarly, not entirely to blame. The truth is that we like getting our news from celebrities. We live in a country where, issue for issue, *Heat*, *Hello* and *OK* regularly outsell *The Guardian*, *The Independent* and *The Times*. Regardless of your definition, all these publications are sources of news, designed to keep their readers up to date and informed. Which one you buy largely depends on what constitutes news to you. To the readers of *Closer* or *Grazia*, what Cheryl Cole, Take That, Simon Cowell or any of this season's *X Factor* contestants are thinking, saying or wearing is just as important as the views of David Cameron, Mervyn King or Shami Chakrabarti are to listeners of the *Today* programme.

PRs find it is much easier to promote a person than a product. People buy people – especially if they're famous. Getting a celebrity to front your campaign – out of the goodness of their heart – will guarantee you more coverage, but the same is true if you pay one to promote your product. People do not necessarily distinguish between these two activities. Whether Nadine Baggott is letting slip yet another beauty secret during an Olay advert or whether she's reviewing beauty products in her column in *Hello*, to the audience, she's the same old Baggott. Any underlying issues of commerce do not concern them. Likewise, whether Stephen Fry is presenting *QI*, eruditely stating the case against the papacy, or persuading you that you really can get a better rate of car insurance with Direct Line, to the audience he is the same Stephen Fry: the actor, the writer, the polymath, the national treasure, never the insurance salesman. Which is, of course, exactly why Direct Line, Arla foods, Tesco, WH Smith, Calor Gas, Orange, Kenco, Virgin, Coca-Cola, Dairylea, Twinings, Walkers, Argos, Trebor-Bassett, Heineken, the Royal Mail, Alliance and Leicester and Imperial Tobacco have all used Stephen Fry to promote their products.

Through PR, the media itself is manipulated. The organisations and brands that engage in PR view the media as nothing more than another communications channel. Certainly one through which the message is more difficult to control than it is through advertising or the company website, but the upside is that if communication is achieved, it is far more powerful.

I can tell you that my book is great, but you'd be much more inclined to believe this fact if it was Stephen Fry telling you. This is why editorial is many times more persuasive than advertising. It looks impartial, but it might not be. You wouldn't know whether I paid the imaginary Stephen Fry to big-up my work or whether his was a genuine endorsement, because the end result would look exactly the same. Was Stephen Fry paid to take part in the debate about the Catholic Church? I assume not, but there is plenty of evidence to suggest he can be paid to say things he doesn't necessarily believe; perhaps this was one of those occasions, how can we tell? Alternatively, are we to accept that he has the same conviction when he's telling you that you can do 'A Good Deal Better' with Direct Line as he does when he's explaining why he believes that the Catholic Church is not a force for good in the world? What about when he's telling us how much he rates Apple in one of his newspaper columns? At the very least, we have to concede that if there is a line somewhere, it's very ill defined.

Whether it's reporting a genuine piece of news or PR, the media doesn't just tell us what is going on in a story; it tells us what to think about it as well. Just as we were told what to think about Philip Laing, we are told how to respond to everything from a Royal Wedding to the England football team's shock World Cup exit.[4]

In the autumn of 2010, the Coalition government launched its Welfare Reform Bill. Its stated aim was to always ensure that employment was a more attractive option than unemployment and, in doing so, rid society of the 'Benefit Culture' that has been holding us back all these years. The plans outlined within it were not to make employment a more attractive option by improving pay and conditions and creating more jobs, but to make unemployment a less attractive option, by removing and reducing benefits, thereby incentivising claimants to find gainful occupation.

In terms of shaping public opinion it was a brilliant strategy. Avoiding the issue of where the jobs for this – one assumes – largely unskilled section of the population are going to come from during the deepest recession for 20 years, it draws a distinction between the feckless, lazy poor and the honest, hard-working poor. Certainly it is much easier for the latter group to relate to somebody they might know who might be a few thousand quid to the good, thanks to a dubious claim for sickness or incapacity benefit, than it is for them to relate to a faceless investment banker

---

[4] Always a shock exit. Despite the fact that, with one exception, England finished somewhere between sixth and thirteenth in every World Cup they've qualified for since 1962. And before you write in and 'have your say' remember England didn't have to qualify in either 1966 or 1970.

who's garnered a multi-million pound bonus for managing their pension fund with slightly less ineptitude than his or her peers. As the debate focused on benefit cheats and malingerers, so the issue of banking reform and bonus restructuring slipped quietly from screens and pages.

Whether we like it or not, through our desire to keep informed, our inclination to engage emotionally rather than rationally, and our simplistic broad worldview, we often end up holding views that are not necessarily our own and which have no basis in fact. In Everything Now this process is so advanced that we can often be persuaded to hold two contradictory views at the same time. And nobody understands this better, or exploits this more adroitly, than the global super-brands.

Chapter 10
The Real Thing

'If I had a world of my own, everything would be nonsense. Nothing would be what it is, because everything would be what it isn't. And contrary wise, what it is, it wouldn't be. And what it wouldn't be, it would. You see?' – *Alice,* Alice in Wonderland

English football underwent many famous changes during the 1990s. It's easy to forget, but the game went into that decade not so much on its knees, as on its belly. In 1989 English clubs were still banned from taking part in European competitions, a result of the Heysel tragedy, and still reeling from the financial implications of the Taylor Report, a result of the Hillsborough tragedy, and its demand for expensive modernisation. It wasn't just the stadia, the whole infrastructure of the game was crumbling; both attendances and revenues were dwindling and a proposed identity card scheme threatened to kill casual support of the sport altogether. On reflection, then, it's even more surprising that a decade that started off by looking like it was going to be football's nadir, turned out instead to be the game's second Golden Age.

It was during the 90s that money started flooding into the game, but a time before foreign ownership of clubs began. Teams consisted of essentially home-based players, supplemented by sometimes dazzling talent from overseas, and the national side reached the semi-finals of two international tournaments. Much has been written about the impact of Italia 90, the Premiership and Sky Sports, but it was also the first time that the clubs started to think of themselves as brands as well as businesses.

The problem with running a football club as a business is

that businesses have to grow and they usually do this by selling more things to more customers. Football clubs don't have any customers: they have supporters and, unfortunately, from a business perspective, this support tends to be ingrained, so it's not easily transferred from club to club. People don't tend to change the team that they support. Some do of course – it might be just me, but there seem to be far more Chelsea fans around today than there were 20 years ago – but for the most part, people pick a club and stick with them through thick and thin. And for most, it will all be thin because every club has its glass ceiling. Sides like Aston Villa or Everton might each have a national fan base of around 500,000 people, but their commitment will range from hardcore at one end – those who travel to every away game – to the latent at the other – those who might occasionally keep an eye on the results in the newspapers. If the club is successful, it will be able to engage with more fans towards the latent end of the spectrum and may be able to extract more revenue from the hardcore, but what it won't be able to do easily is to attract new supporters. Even if my hunch about Chelsea is true, and this can be achieved by effectively buying trophies, then the cost of attracting these additional fans runs into hundreds of millions of pounds: sums of money that are simply not available to most football clubs, even comparatively large ones like Aston Villa or Everton.

It was a problem that appeared to have no solution, until 1995 when Manchester United decided to solve it. United realised that the problem only existed while you allowed yourself to be fettered by national boundaries and historic local rivalries. If you can't attract new British fans, why not build up a following overseas instead? United had long been one of the most famous clubs in the world, but now it moved to exploit that popularity for the first time by proactively growing its support in foreign territories. The club established a new division, Manchester United International, to help achieve this. The venture, under the stewardship of managing director Michael Farnan and the watchful eye of CEO Peter

Kenyon, was highly successful. The business witnessed substantial growth from merchandise sales in Asia, the Middle East and Australasia over the next few years, on the back of successful, high-profile summer tours by the first team. The club also rolled out, opening retail stores and Red Cafes across the world, under the auspices of 'Bringing Old Trafford to the fans'.

It was a model that many clubs tried to replicate, but few succeeded. The reason for Manchester United's triumph was not simply that it was first, or that it was better or even more successful than anyone else. The reason is that, like all great brands, it was able to make an emotional connection with many people across the globe who, despite not even knowing where Manchester was, believed that one of its football teams had 'something' to say to them and offered membership of 'something' they wanted to be a part of. Understanding how this emotional connection is made and what that 'something' is are the keys to understanding how branding works.

We all know what a brand is and, if asked, I'm sure we could comfortably rattle off the names of several dozen, but branding itself is something of a dark art. Even though we know one when we see it, coming up with a definition for what a brand actually is is something of a challenge. The first thing to make clear is that brands are not the same thing as logos. A logo is a graphic mark or emblem, used to provide instant recognition for a company, organisation, event or individual. Logos can be used to focus our attention, but they are not brands themselves any more than flags are countries or club badges are football teams. So if a brand is not a logo, what is it? The marketing textbook definition will be some variation on the following:

> A brand is a product, service, or concept that is publicly distinguished from other products, services or concepts so that it can be easily communicated and marketed.

Business author, Seth Godin, offers a more conceptual definition:

> A brand is the set of expectations, memories, stories and relationships that, taken together, account for a consumer's decision to choose one product or service over another. If the consumer (whether it's a business, a buyer, a voter or a donor) doesn't pay a premium, make a selection or spread the word, then no brand value exists for that consumer.

These two descriptions are helpful in terms of understanding what a brand is, and Godin's interpretation comes close to the essence of what makes a brand, but neither really explains how branding works. For example, why can some products be 'distinguished' – turned into brands – while others can't? Nor do they explain how and why our relationship with branded goods differs from that with equally useful unbranded products.

One thing we can agree on is that successful branding is about making a product, company or service stand out from the crowd: it's about being different. Brands are simply concepts that we connect with on an emotional level. Indeed, like deciding which music we like, there is very little that is rational about our relationship with brands.

Research into consumer attitudes towards branding reveals views that are quite often contradictory. Respondents typically say they like brands because they are a guarantee of quality that can be trusted, but at the same time will be quite cynical towards them because they feel they are overpriced and oversold. When we love brands, it is because they seem to offer us something unique and authentic, something that we want, and in doing so they seem to be speaking to us directly. You can see this in the language we use to describe brands we like, which is usually informal and personal. We talk of 'trusted brands' or 'quality brands'; we show 'brand loyalty'; and we even give them little nicknames: eat at Macky

D's, shop at Primani or Harvey Nic's, drive a Beamer, watch the Beeb, or drink a Bud. Powerful brands can achieve a notoriety that exceeds their entire category. We drink Coke or Pepsi, not cola; we watch Sky TV, not satellite TV. Fans of the Apple brand don't buy laptops, MP3 players or mobile phones; they buy Macbooks, iPods or iPhones (and generally spend a lot of their spare time telling the rest of the world how great they are).

Brands have personality. Volvo is safe; Innocent is caring; Virgin is a bit irreverent and Apple is cool in a way that Microsoft just isn't. In our broad worldview the concept of what Alfa Romeo or BMW stand for is just as well formed as our concept of what Jeremy Clarkson or Richard Hammond stand for. In turn, to the people they connect with, Jeremy Clarkson and a 3 Series BMW become more than just an opinionated motor journalist and a popular family saloon. They become something that intuitively feels bigger and more authentic, yet indescribable and intangible all at the same time.

Even when the product is the same, the brand personality can be completely different. Apple and Dell are both computer companies that make high-quality products and both have very strong brand personalities. Yet Apple is synonymous with innovation and Dell isn't. The difference is not in what they do – both are computer companies with similar structures, and both are committed to making great products. The difference is in consumers' perception of why they do it, and how they relate to that. Consumers perceive that Apple is committed to taking risks, beautiful design and finding innovative ways to do familiar things: whether it's listening to music, watching a movie, using a mobile phone or surfing the Internet. Dell is committed to making great PCs. If I simply want a great PC, I'll probably buy a Dell, because it'll do everything a Mac does and it's a lot cheaper. If I want to believe there's a better way of doing things (whether or not there actually is, is irrelevant) and I think that's cool and I want to be a part of it, I'll buy a Mac.

Even if Dell and Apple were to release two identical products simultaneously, they would still be perceived as different. This 'certain something' that gives a brand its unique personality can be infuriatingly difficult to identify, but there is no denying that it can produce feelings within all of us that are immensely compelling.

Brands work by exploiting two fundamental human instincts. During the aforementioned football revolution of the 90s, my focus was squarely on the rump of the English League. At that time my own team, Wigan Athletic, was in the bottom flight, with a terrible ground and crowds of less than 2,000. It wasn't the Premiership 'Giant' that it went on to become and most of the time it didn't feel like we were standing in a hurricane of modernisation, but change was taking place. Watching football was generally much safer than it had been in the 80s, away fans were no longer treated as guilty until proven innocent and the clubs had started waking up to the fact that they were in the entertainment business. One of the signs that things were really beginning to change was the re-emergence of the club mascot.

Clubs have always had mascots, but they were regarded as something exclusively for the kids – if, that is, they were ever regarded at all. These 90s versions might have started with much the same intentions – to create something that would appeal to the children and perhaps lead fans in a bit of singing – but the execution was completely different. Usually consisting of a huge bespoke costume of some cartoon animal, with a name that was either alliterative (Filbert the Fox, Harry the Hornet) or a pun (Gunnersaurus Rex, Roary the Lion) or both (Lucas the Kop Kat) or neither (Toby the Wyvern) these mascots were operated by individuals whose personality was somewhere on the spectrum between extreme extrovert and borderline psychotic. They behaved in a manner that went beyond the emphatic, often bordering on an incitement to riot.[5]

[5] The mascots were often more entertaining than the games. In 2003 Swansea mascot Cyril the Swan was fined £1,000 for removing the head of Millwall's Zampa the Lion and drop-kicking it across the ground with a shout of 'Don't fuck with the Swans!'

My favourite mascot was Hartlepool United's H'Angus the Monkey. H'Angus was evicted from away grounds on a number of occasions. His reputation went before him and once, during a 2001 game at Scunthorpe United, he was thrown out simply because a steward objected to the vigour with which H'Angus was leading the faithful in song. He was immensely popular with supporters, so much so that in 2002, he became Hartlepool's first democratically elected mayor.

This event had a beautiful dramatic irony. H'Angus's name derives from an incident that allegedly took place during the Napoleonic war. A French ship was wrecked off the Northumberland coast and the only survivor was a monkey, which had been dressed – presumably for the late crew's entertainment – in French military uniform. Unfortunately for the poor animal, the good people of Hartlepool had seen neither a monkey nor a Frenchman before. On the basis that the monkey was dressed as a Frenchman and couldn't understand or speak English, they assumed that he was a French spy. He was summarily tried, found guilty of espionage and sentenced to death. The original H'Angus was hanged from the mast of a fishing boat the same day. In 200 years Hartlepool had gone from hanging monkeys to electing them to office, a remarkable feat of restitution by anyone's standards.

As rational, educated people, it's hard not to laugh at the attempts to either put a monkey on trial or to elect it to public office, but we shouldn't be so quick to judge the citizens of Hartlepool past or present. The people involved in both cases were falling victim to an irrational trait that affects us all much more than we think.

Anthropomorphism is something almost all of us engage in every day. Most pet owners give their animals names, many talk to them and some buy them presents on their birthdays. You may have yelled at your mobile phone, cursed your computer or told that little Paperclip Man (who used to pop up uninvited whenever you opened Microsoft Word) what he could do with his false

126

promises of help. The famous scene in *Fawlty Towers*, where Basil dishes out a 'damn good thrashing' to his Austin 1100, is funny because we can all relate to his frustrations with malfunctioning machines.

Anthropomorphism is ingrained in human nature. Some of the oldest cave art depicts the chimera: a shamanic entity that was half-man, half-beast, suggesting that the trait has been around for tens of thousands of years. Anthropomorphic figures from nature are also abundant in folklore: dryads, nymphs and sylphs were female spirits of woods, water and air. Others like Mother Nature and Jack Frost are still widely in use today. Anthropologists believe we are hard-wired to see human-like beings and qualities everywhere, but although the phenomenon is widespread and profound, it remained ignored and unstudied until the turn of this century, when the growing popularity of virtual environments found in video games led to widespread interaction with avatars and non-human entities.

The most successful of these games are the ones that exploit our propensity to anthropomorphise. *Football Manager* is one of the most popular franchises of the past twenty years. Players take on the role of a football manager, looking after the training, player development, team selection and tactics of their chosen club. In reality, these 'players' have been reduced to nothing more than a spreadsheet of statistics for several dozen attributes such as passing, tackling, pace and fitness. Yet any one of the millions of people who have played this game will tell you that it is remarkably immersive, to the extent that you do begin to care about these lines of statistics as if they were real people. You start wondering how to get the best out of a star striker, whether to rest your first choice centre-back, or whether your out-of-form team captain is becoming unsettled since you relegated him to the reserves. On more than one occasion, I've felt sorry for my once cherished, but now overlooked full-back mouldering away in the reserves and given him a game in the League Cup, just to keep his spirits up.

Psychologists have tried to find out what exactly happens inside our heads when we anthropomorphise in this way and how it evolved. One popular theory is that it's a by-product of using our own preferences to predict how someone else will react to a comment or action. How well will they respond to this story? Will they like the present we've got them? Will they be offended if we don't go? And so on. From here, it's a small step to using the same processes to divine the thoughts of animals or even objects. And, just as we build complex emotional relationships with human personalities we don't know, so we do with non-human personalities. We call them brands.

As well as our propensity to anthropomorphise, brands also exploit the manner in which the human mind calculates value. We often pursue authenticity as an end in itself. Paintings and sculpture are an obvious example where an original is worth many times more than an identical copy, but there are millions of collectors who will pay a premium for ordinary objects because they have an extraordinary history. For example, a pen that was used by Churchill is more valuable than an identical pen that wasn't. Again, this quality is intangible: the pen itself undergoes no physical metamorphosis as a result of being used by Churchill, but in our view it is changed forever as a result of its association with him. That is why, in experiments where people have been asked to choose between two identical items, one featuring a recognised brand while the other is entirely unbranded, the vast majority choose the branded item. The choice has nothing to do with functionality – remember, both items are identical – it is down to the perceived authenticity offered by the brand, which is ultimately an emotional, not a rational decision.

In this way, branding helps us to distinguish between product X and product Y when there is absolutely no difference between them. Your choice of soap powder illustrates this point very well. I imagine that you probably demonstrate some kind of brand loyalty in this area. Do you always buy Persil? Or perhaps you're a Daz household or an Ariel couple? Are you a powder or liquid user? Do you combine your powder with a fabric conditioner? I also assume you can explain your purchasing decision – is your powder cheaper? Does it wash whiter than white? Maybe it's kind to colours or perhaps tough on grease and grime? Now here are three points to consider: Are your clothes actually any cleaner than your friends' and colleagues'? Can you tell what washing powder somebody uses just by looking at his or her clean clothes? Can you tell when somebody uses the same brand as you? Thought not.

In 2007, research carried out by psychologists Bruce Hood and Paul Bloom showed that we are all born with this instinct to value authenticity. In one experiment, 43 children between the ages of 3 and 6 were shown a tachistoscope that had been jazzed up with flashing lights and buzzers, and told that it was a 'copying machine' which could reproduce a perfect copy of any object. After a short demonstration, the children were told it could also make perfect replicas of toys. A doll was placed into the machine and a duplicate was produced. When the children were then asked which one they would prefer, 62 percent chose the duplicate. The doll's authenticity was not an issue for them. Next, the kids were asked to place an attachment object into the machine (such as a favourite toy or teddy) that the scientists would copy for them. None of the children would accept that the duplicate was the equivalent of the original object, despite reassurances by the researchers that they were identical in every way. When asked why they felt that way, the children talked about the new items lacking the sentimental bond and personal history of the originals.

The same is true when it comes to brands. We stop having favourite toys, but we never get beyond our emotional desire for essentialism and authenticity. For brands, it is their legitimacy that gives them their value. We may be happy to watch a pirated movie on our Sony Vaio, but we want the laptop we are watching it on to be the real deal. This is because when we see the logo, we don't just see a font or a marque and we certainly don't see the product itself; what we do is connect emotionally with a concept that is unique: there might be billions of teddies in the world, but there is only one 'Teddy'.

When we start to engage emotionally, there is no room – nor need – for rationality. The genius of Everything Now is that brands no longer need to respond to actual needs; they can create the needs themselves and then develop a product that responds to them.

As we have seen, raising awareness of public health issues surrounding food will not necessarily make us eat any more healthily, let alone make us experts on nutrition. What it succeeds in doing is raising awareness that we probably can't eat whatever we want without consequences, thereby instilling us with the vague notion that some foods are good for us and some aren't. This creates an opportunity. Imagine if somebody were to launch a food product that tasted great, was fun to eat, could be eaten every day and was actually good for us – surely such a product would fly off the shelves.

The probiotic drinks market – populated by brands like Actimel and Yakult – is worth over £220 million in the UK alone. These yogurt-based drinks contain bacteria and are good for us – or so we are told. But how exactly are they good for us? The manufacturers don't make any outlandish claims, they're not promising immortality, longevity or even a disease-free existence. The advertising for Actimel merely asks, 'Have you had your Actimel today?' This implies that drinking the yogurt makes for a healthier lifestyle, but the question we seldom ask is, healthier in relation to what? If these drinks are good for you, then it is only in the same way that a banana is, or a carrot (or any other of your five portions a day for that matter) and in a way that processed food, like probiotic yogurt, usually isn't. Whatever the truth is, in the UK alone, without ever really questioning why, we end up buying more than 150,000 probiotic yogurt drinks every day.

Marketers no longer need to make the message clear. Their job was once to create a rational, differentiated proposition based on product benefits and customer insights ('You want a soap powder that gets your sheets white? Did you know that Persil washes whiter?'), but now the best results are achieved by taking a more abstract approach.

Chocolate bars are what marketers describe as an impulse purchase: a decision to buy a product that is unplanned. Impulse purchases are motivated exclusively by emotions and feelings; we see chocolate bars on sale by the checkout and suddenly we decide we want one. Some people may have a favourite bar, but most of us will stare at the array of brightly packaged treats until one suggests itself to us. The job of the chocolate marketer is to make sure that it's their bar that pops into mind in the split second it takes us to decide which one to buy.

In 2007, Cadbury launched an advertising campaign to promote its Dairy Milk brand. The 90-second commercial, produced by the Fallon Agency of London, was a true example of that much over-used term: surrealism. It featured a 400 lb gorilla, clearly thinking he was having the best time ever, playing the drums to 'In the Air Tonight' by Phil Collins, with the strapline 'A glass and a half full of joy'. The campaign was hugely successful and sales of Dairy Milk soared, but what was this advert trying to tell us about the product? The answer is: nothing.

Fallon claims that the creative was 'founded upon the notion that all communications should be as effortlessly enjoyable as eating the bar itself', but you'd have to dig in pretty deep to get that message out and it doesn't sound like a good opener for a water cooler conversation either. Nevertheless, sales of Dairy Milk went through the roof.

The reason the campaign succeeded is because it told us something about ourselves. We all like to think of ourselves as being a little bit out of the ordinary, not just like everybody else and definitely not run-of-the-mill, so when we see something that's sort of edgy, sort of funny, sort of weird, sort of cool, sort of out of the ordinary, but ultimately, sort of safe as well, we respond very positively. And the next time we're at the sweetie counter, guess which brand first comes to mind? This kind of reinforcement is by its nature ephemeral. Several years later and it's going to take more than a drumming gorilla to persuade you to choose a bar of Dairy Milk – but there will be another idea along the way, with perhaps a retro-science theme or dancing eyebrows.

This kind of communication is not unique to chocolate. In a 2004 survey, when consumers were asked their views about TV advertisements to promote the telecoms companies Vodaphone and Orange, over 80 percent of respondents said that they had no idea what the ads were trying to tell them. This doesn't mean that they were ineffective: it just means that the ads weren't trying to tell them anything. Instead they were trying to give the sense of something positive, something good, something empowering, something cool, but ultimately something vague, about owning a mobile phone on a particular network. It is far easier to do this than it is to empirically differentiate your product from one by your competitor, which is, to all intents and purposes, identical. Vodaphone, Orange, O2, T-Mobile, 3: when it boils down to it, they are simply holders of exactly the same license to sell airtime on the same network. Really what possible difference could there be?

Branding is often the only difference between competing products within the same category, but what a difference it is. Coca-Cola and Pepsi Cola are virtually identical in chemical composition, yet people routinely display a strong preference for one or the other. A 2004 study into how our perception of the brands shapes our preferences was carried out at the Baylor College of Medicine in Houston, USA. In the experiment, one group of subjects was given Coke and Pepsi anonymously, without any branding or indication as to which was which, while the second group was given branded versions of the two colas to try. During the tasting, the subjects were given MRI scans to determine if anything different was happening in their brains. In the anonymous task, the scans revealed that this group was relying exclusively upon sensory information to inform their preference. Scans for the group given branded products, revealed something completely different was going on. This group was using other parts of the brain to arrive at their decision, most notably the hippocampus, which plays an important role in the formation of new memories about experienced events. The results showed that the subjects' brand knowledge was biasing their decisions to such an extent that it was actually overriding sensory information. In essence, we prefer a particular brand because we think we'll prefer it, not because we actually do.

When we stroll down the supermarket aisles, with several thousand different brands on display, it is easy to reach out and put whichever seems to be speaking to us into our basket, without stopping to consider why we're doing it. The next time you're out shopping, try asking yourself why you've chosen this particular item in your hand over all the others, you'll be surprised how difficult it is to come up with an answer. The ubiquity of branding has led our economy to become increasingly concept-based. Success is not about developing a great product – that's merely the ticket price, without a great product there's no point in trying to take it to market – it is about establishing a great brand. This process of selling concepts is epitomised by companies like Adidas, Coke and Orange who are entirely devoted to persuading us to choose between competing sets of nebulous lifestyle choices. The emergence of digital media has allowed this concept-based economy to expand; in the process we have become, unwittingly, the most effective members of the brands' marketing departments.

Chapter 11
Have Your Say:
Why Your Opinion Is Important to Us

'Narcissus does not fall in love with his reflection because it is beautiful, but because it is his.' – *W. H. Auden, poet*

With so many brands competing for our attention, we are made to feel that what we think matters, that our opinions are valuable and noteworthy. We are constantly asked to 'Have Your Say' as if the brands require our counsel before deciding what their next move should be. But with so much information being pumped out, communication has now become an objective as well as a process. We might find it easy to have our say, but the question is, is anyone actually listening?

Talk is cheap. For schedulers and editors wrestling with the conundrum of increasing amounts of airtime and column inches to fill, versus decreasing budgets with which to fill them, the words of readers and listeners provide a tantalising trove of free editorial. Like a well that never runs dry, the willingness of the public to Have Your Say is the only thing keeping many media outlets in business. Where would Talk Radio or 5 Live be without their legion of unpaid, amateur analysts? How would *The X Factor* or *Britain's Got Talent* survive without their hoards of unpaid, amateur performers or armies of unpaid, amateur A&Rs, phoning in to pass judgement on tonight's performances? And what would become of Facebook or Twitter or WordPress without the tweeters, posters and bloggers and their status updates and opinion pieces?

User Generated Content (UGC) is the rather ugly term for this and many other kinds of amateur contribution. The phrase has only recently entered common usage, but it has become a catch-all, covering a wide range of applications from news articles by citizen journalists, to gossip, reviews and pithier comments found at the foot of online magazine articles. It is also used to describe all the emerging new media technologies: digital video sites, blogs, podcasts, forums, news groups, review sites, social networking sites, photography portals and the various wikis and other open source projects that abound online. Websites like Facebook, Twitter and MySpace rely almost exclusively on UGC, while for others, such as Amazon, YouTube or the various news portals, it forms only part of the offer.

UGC is not exclusive to the web. There are the aforementioned radio and TV phone-ins, but newspapers and magazines also dedicate a considerable amount of space to stories provided by their readers. If you've got something to say, you're not short of platforms from which to say it. In fact, UGC has become so widespread that if you're willing to put in a little effort (like making sure you're one of the first to comment on an article or becoming a regular caller to a phone-in show) then you can easily reach an audience of hundreds of thousands without spending much more than a few quid.

Throughout the Internet's brief but tempestuous history, this vast, alternative, amateur media's battle for legitimacy has been a recurring story in itself. Those controlling the purse strings at professional media outlets have embraced amateur editorial in the interests of commerce, but while their publications, programmes and channels reap the benefits of free content, and the creators themselves enjoy the opportunity to reach a wider audience, the professional writers and journalists have been much less enthusiastic, finding their ability to draw down a living wage hampered by the acceptance of poorly crafted, scantily researched and cursorily edited work.

Their case is encapsulated in the book *Flat Earth News*. Written by *Guardian* journalist Nick Davies, it provides a thorough, well-researched and compelling account of the failings, and qualitative decline, of the mass media in general and newspapers in particular. Davies argues that commercial pressures have made the job of accurate reporting almost impossible. Journalists, forced to cut corners, rely more and more upon partisan sources of information to provide the basis for their stories; notably, the PR departments and communications teams acting on behalf of large organisations. Davies' analysis of the decline of probity within, what he terms, 'the quality media' is poignant and heartfelt, but it has even wider implications when one considers that fewer people than ever rely upon traditional outlets for their information.

Taken as a whole – a whole made up of myriad, fragmented parts, to be sure – the audience for amateur content is vast. For many, it is now their primary source of news. This begs the question; from where are these amateurs getting their information? One might like to believe that the blogs, podcasts and forums are authored by individuals with the inside track on their particular area of expertise, or at least access to a coterie of company insiders, willing to spill the beans on what is really happening. The truth is much more prosaic. Having been an insider at several big companies, I can honestly say that what sensitive information there is has usually been known by a very small number of people with corporate communication tightly and effectively managed by the PR departments. It is their PR announcements that are the invisible source for almost every news item you read online. Granted, this is not always the case, but for every WikiLeaks there are literally tens of thousands of blogs where it is.

Just like Newton's laws of motion, the commercial realities of generating editorial are universal. One 500-word article looks very much the same as another on the page or screen, but the costs of putting it together can vary enormously. Executing an exposé of corporate corruption, or an elaborate sting, can be an expensive undertaking often involving days, or even weeks, of potentially fruitless endeavour. On the other hand, a write-up of your opinion of a film, news item or TV show, filling the same column inches, can be knocked out in half an hour, while cutting and pasting a press release with a bit of analysis topping and tailing is a matter of minutes. In media terms, nothing is cheaper than opinion and analysis, it requires no research, no time-consuming chase for quotes from third parties and often, judging by a lot of the results, no consideration either.

With so much of it about and access so easy, we can forget that this kind of public expression was practically impossible 20 years ago. The BBC only began its daytime broadcast service in 1986. It needed cheap content to fill the schedules and, along with the Australian soap operas and cheesy Euro-quizzes, commissioned a new early-mid-morning show called *Open Air*. Hosted by Eamonn Holmes, the programme was similar in format to Channel 4's *Right to Reply* or the BBC's *Points of View* and invited viewers to have their say about the previous evening's viewing. The difference was that *Open Air* was live, so that viewers didn't just write in their say, they could phone in and have their say live on air.

The phone-in itself was not an 80s invention. The first UK phone-in was broadcast by Radio Nottingham in 1968 as a segment in a programme called *What Are They Up To Now?* In the late 70s Noel Edmonds launched *Swap Shop*, which invited viewers to call in ('Remember to dial 01 if you're outside London') with items they wished to swap ('A Barbie doll for anything on Abba') or to put questions to one of the celebrity guests. In the McKevitt household, that '01 if you're outside London' bit was effectively the final nail in our Have Your Say coffin. Not only did my dad rule that the cost of the long-distance phone call would be prohibitively expensive, but he also went to great lengths to assure us that any transgression would constitute a capital offence. Another avenue of pleasure closed off to us, we ended up watching the phone-in free *Tiswas* instead.

Not that any of our friends with better telecom freedoms were able to build a bigger media profile for themselves. Not only did we not know anybody who managed to get a call live on air, but we didn't know anybody who knew anybody who'd managed to get a call through either. An ordinary member of the public who wished to appear on TV or radio had essentially just three options at this time. They could apply to become a game show contestant, they could commit a serious criminal act or, if that was too extreme, they could do something embarrassing or eccentric – like playing the recorder with your nose, or riding a unicycle to work – and attempt to secure a slot on either *That's Life* or *Nationwide*.

Access to the media improved dramatically once I left school and started sixth-form college. First of all, ITV launched a teatime game show called *Blockbusters*, where the contestants were all sixth-form pupils. Further proof of the reality of this media opportunity was provided when one of my mates, Martin McDonald, managed to get himself on the show for the best part of a week (and netting himself four Gold Runs, an adventure holiday in North Wales and 250 quid). Secondly, our local independent radio station Red Rose FM, started broadcasting a daily, late-night radio phone-in. *The Allan Beswick Late Night Show* was hosted by the titular Beswick, a curmudgeonly but erudite Lancastrian. The format was simple. Listeners were invited to ring in and Have Your Say after which, Beswick would argue with them – usually quite vehemently. He had a flair for playing devil's advocate, often taking contrary positions in consecutive phone calls and his show quickly developed a cult following, which included my friends and I̶ me.

The other good thing about the show was that it broadcast from Preston not London – which meant any calls we made to the show would be local rate and therefore wouldn't show up on the itemised bill. Add in the fact that it aired at a time when my mum was likely to be in bed and my dad likely to be down the pub, and we now had both unfettered access to the BT phone network, and a theoretical opportunity to broadcast live to the region. Getting through to the show was one thing, but knowing

138

that all your mates were listening in, and would be discussing your performance the following day, was the real prize.

Our group's star caller was The Impressionist John Culshaw (although while we were at sixth-form he was just known as John Culshaw). He did do impressions though. All the time. John would usually ring up as 'Arthur from Ormskirk' and do a highly accurate, but relatively obscure impression of sci-fi author Arthur C. Clarke and demand to speak about some kind of paranormal phenomena. He was usually given short shrift, with Beswick no doubt as bemused as most of the listeners, but not before he'd managed to slip in a few catchphrases from the TV series *Arthur C. Clarke's Mysterious World*. Even if no one else did, our corner of the common room found it hilarious. Perhaps we could have put this platform to better use, but personally, I doubt it.

Along with the phone-ins, another pillar of the daytime schedules was the studio audience participation debate. BBC1's *Kilroy* and Anglia TV's *The Time The Place* pioneered this ugly format with an ugly name. Both shows initially took a topical issue and invited the audience to Have Your Say, but over time, the topics became less political and current affairs based, and increasingly concerned with human interest stories. Studio debates, like *The Jeremy Kyle Show*, remain a hugely popular component of today's daytime schedule, albeit considerably more prurient in tone.

The launch of the BBC's 24/7 rolling news station Radio 5 Live in March 1994 created further demand for content generated by the audience. Phone-ins were an integral part of the schedule. 5 Live's *606*, where sports fans are invited to Have Your Say, has spawned countless copies, while the station's daily *Your Call* show gives callers the biggest platform in the UK and the opportunity to reach a potential 6.75 million listeners.

It may have been unheard of prior to 1996, but User Generated Content shows no sign of going out of fashion. There are 24 million users of Facebook in the UK, all of them generating some form of content, and while Twitter's popularity has been overplayed by the media, there are still 2 million tweeters who can have their say pithily in less than 140 characters.

Now, having teed up the phenomenon of User Generated Content, you might be expecting me to whack it down the fairway with the 4-iron of contempt. The truth is I don't think there is anything intrinsically wrong or bad about any of this. I admire Nick Davies and agree with his analysis, but I don't entirely share his lament. As George Orwell once said, 'Early in life I had noticed that no event is ever correctly reported in a newspaper.' That's not to trivialise the pursuit of The Truth, or the efforts of many journalists, but rather to recognise the fact that, despite their best endeavours, the purpose of all the publications, papers or programmes they work for is to deliver an audience to its advertisers and thereby a profit for its owners.

A free press is a vital component of a democracy, but most media outlets operate within 'free' parameters set by their owners. The courtship of News International owner Rupert Murdoch, by both leading UK political parties, is testament to this. In that sense, if in no other, the Internet's empowerment of previously voiceless individuals to have their say and publish what they want, when they want and with ease, must be lauded. Certainly, the Chinese government's ultimately futile efforts to mitigate the simplicity with which information can be exchanged online within its borders demonstrates how difficult and costly it has now become to control what people say about you.

Likewise, I have no issue with anyone wanting to update friends, family or acquaintances on their comings and goings. Nor do I believe that the fact that there are now thousands of young girls talking about themselves on webcams, and posting the results on their own YouTube channels, heralds the end of civilisation. And if someone wants to spend time writing a blog to let us know their take on the situation in the Middle East, what they think about European fiscal policy, or to share their opinion of a hotel, restaurant, book or film, then good luck to them. The fact is people have always liked talking about themselves and sharing information, it's just that they've never had the opportunity to do it so extensively before.

With something as broad as UGC, there is always going to be an up and downside. Websites like eBay, TripAdvisor and Facebook have had a largely benign impact on their users' lives, making the process of such diverse lifestyle challenges as buying and selling second-hand goods, planning a foreign holiday and keeping in touch with family and friends as easy as clicking a mouse. The fact that these sites are also occasionally used to post inaccurate reviews, rip customers off or bully people is a sad but inevitable consequence of the freedom of access.

Access to the media is now ubiquitous. Unlike us, our children are growing up in a world that is truly connected and, in the process, what was once astonishing to us, has become ordinary and unremarkable to them. One of the biggest shows on TV during my teenage years in the early 80s was *Surprise Surprise*. It was a primetime, Sunday night vehicle for Cilla Black – strangely, the biggest star of the time – and it regularly pulled an audience of more than 15 million people. As the title implies, the show surprised people, usually working-class people, because they were rarely seen on TV in those days and were relatively easy to surprise. A doughty pensioner would get a day out in London and return home to find they had been given – surprise surprise – a new kitchen; a dedicated care worker would get a trip to Disneyland and return home to find – surprise surprise – they had been given a new kitchen; or a tired mum would be given a makeover and return home to find she'd been given – surprise surprise… you get the idea.

The show's most popular item, saved for the big finale, consisted of long-lost family members being reunited across the continents usually by live satellite link-up. Long lost brothers and sisters, mothers and sons, friends and relatives were all reunited live on television in front of millions of viewers. It's impossible to imagine an item like this working on television today. Now, it would be more surprising if anyone lost touch at all, unless they really wanted to. Maintaining your anonymity is the biggest challenge: a feat that requires a considerable amount of dedication and complete social media-asceticism in order to pull off.

It is this connectivity and readiness to exchange information that makes UGC so ripe for exploitation. Asking somebody to tell you what they think used to be one of the biggest compliments you could ever pay them. An opinion is like an appendix: everybody's got one, but that doesn't mean they're any use; however if someone asks for your opinion, well, that's different. It implies that they respect you enough to attach an importance to what you have to say; that, at the very least, they will give what you think some consideration and perhaps even use it to inform their own decisions. I can remember the first time my boss asked me what I thought. It was during a meeting and I felt suddenly empowered, as if I'd ceased to be a mere cog in the machine, that my opinion mattered to him and the team. I don't know if I'd be so excited if that happened today, when it seems like we are being asked for our opinion all the time.

A key consideration for those in charge of commissioning new programmes on TV and radio is the strength of their 'cross-platform strategy'. In other words, how will the format work with mobile phones and other online platforms and how can money be made out of this? *Big Brother* was one of the cross-platform pioneers. Not only was it a huge success on TV, but it also succeeded in persuading millions of people to visit the website and pay money to vote someone out or to receive paid-for content via their mobile phone. This is why every live TV or radio show seems to contain at least one segment that lets viewers Have Your Say – inviting contributions by phone, text or email – in fact, some of the most popular shows do nothing else.

Radio 5 Live's aforementioned *Your Call* is one of these. Effectively the modern equivalent of *The Allan Beswick Late Night*

Show, it is broadcast daily at 9.00am as the final segment of the *Breakfast Show*. It is usually hosted by Nicky Campbell, who is also the station's breakfast show presenter. In essence the format is as follows: Campbell poses topical questions and invites listeners to Have Your Say by joining in the debate with one or two studio guests who will represent opposing sides. One of these guests will usually have a first-hand experience to relate. Broadcasters claim this represents 'the human angle' and while it certainly adds colour, and no doubt encourages listeners to call in, it is questionable whether these kind of anecdotes can ever provide clarity.

A typical example, broadcast on 16 December 2010, was inspired by comments made in an interview with the BBC by former Home Office minister Bob Ainsworth. Talking candidly about his time in office, when his portfolio included Drugs and Organised Crime, Ainsworth said he realised quickly that winning the so-called war on drugs was impossible:

> Leaving the drugs market in the hands of criminals causes huge and unnecessary harms to individuals, communities and entire countries, with the poor the hardest hit... It is time to replace our failed war on drugs with a strict system of legal regulation, to make the world a safer, healthier place, especially for our children.

He also pointed out that billions of pounds had been spent 'without preventing the wide availability of drugs'. Ainsworth was well aware that this would be construed as a fairly radical solution to the drugs problem, but although he expected public antipathy, he knew that, privately, many of those closest to the problem shared his views: 'If I was now a shadow minister, Ed Miliband would be asking me to resign. If one of David Cameron's ministers – despite the fact [the Prime Minister] probably agrees with me – agreed publicly with me, he would have to resign.' Ainsworth said it was fear of a media-fuelled outrage that prevented politicians from arguing for change and that a 'grown-up debate' was needed.

Bob Ainsworth is no radical libertarian, nor do his views put him out on a limb. There is an overwhelming weight of research to support his position that decriminalisation might provide a genuine solution. Many of the health issues associated with drug abuse are a direct consequence of their illegality. There is also consensus among healthcare professionals that legalisation would make these problems much easier to manage. None of this suggests in the slightest that taking drugs is a good thing, or an activity that should be condoned, let alone encouraged; that's certainly not what Ainsworth was saying. His point was that, perhaps, given the fact that the strategy we've been trying for 20 years isn't working and never has, we should consider trying something else to control the drug abuse. He was so bold as to throw an idea into the ring, but what he really wanted was the opportunity to have a mature (i.e. rational) debate; an attempt to explore all the options in the hope of solving what he understands is a highly emotive issue. What problem, you might think, could anyone have with that?

One hour prior to the phone-in, Campbell hosts a studio discussion between two guests about the points raised by Ainsworth. Not only does this more formal debate add an additional angle to the former minister's comments, but it also serves as grist to the mill, encouraging listeners to call in and Have Your Say once the phone lines open. Today's guests are Paul Mendell, a QC who shares much the same view as Ainsworth, and Debra Bell, a mother whose son is suffering from cannabis-induced psychosis.

With this kind of set-up, which is entirely typical, what follows is rarely an informed, well-reasoned, unemotional and balanced exploration of the key issues. What we get instead is an argument; moreover, an argument of the sort that Richard Dawkins will be familiar with, where one side has an emotional basis and the other a rational basis, which, as we have seen, is no sort of contest at all.

Campbell's role, in much the same manner as Beswick's, is not to moderate, but to provoke. He too plays the role of devil's advocate, under the auspices of 'only saying what the listeners are thinking' (a phrase he repeats quite often). Today's discussion begins with Campbell politely asking Mendell to 'outline the arguments in favour of legalisation', which he does. Mendell believes that the current system isn't working. He is calling for an evidence-based, dispassionate discussion to consider alternatives. He says that it is important that the current system is viewed as a benchmark so that the effectiveness of any proposed alternatives can be measured against it. In response, Campbell accuses him of being a secret pro-legaliser, saying that Mendell doesn't really want a debate at all. Mendell spends the rest of the interview protesting defensively that he's not a secret pro-legaliser and that he really does want an unemotional debate.

Campbell then invites Bell to 'tell her story'. The juxtaposition between this invitation and the previous one to 'outline the arguments' serves to highlight the contrast between emotional and rational positions of the respective guests. Bell's story is undoubtedly tragic, but quickly emerges as irrelevant. Given the fact that her son developed his condition under the present system, it's difficult to understand why she's so keen to defend it. If anything, one might expect her to provide further support to Mendell's contention that we need to try something else. But Bell is not interested in defending anything. She is angry and frustrated, and like many people suffering that emotional combination, there is no real focus to her ire. She lashes out at Mendell, accusing 'people like him' of giving 'a green light to children listening to go out and experiment with drugs'. She asks him if anyone in his family has ever suffered a cannabis-induced psychosis? The lawyer replies that no, they haven't, but that this is not about personal issues, it's about a much bigger problem. 'Actually,' Bell responds smugly, 'it's about families!' We never find out what she meant by that comment, because at this point Campbell calls an end to the debate.

With all this key learning digested, Campbell begins the phone-in by posing a question: 'Imagine a world were drugs are legal... How would that work?' His justification is that some of the people calling for decriminalisation – like Bob Ainsworth – 'haven't thought it through'. Without irony, he then asks listeners to call in and Have Your Say. If one is left wondering how many of the show's listeners will have 'thought it through', then the answer is provided immediately by the first caller of the day, Mike from Edgeware, who begins by saying, 'I don't know a great deal about the drugs scene in this country, but...' And it's pretty much downhill from there.

Your Call is not designed to let anyone Have Your Say. In *Flat Earth News*, Davies contends that journalists are in pursuit of the truth. Certainly I'd agree that some of them are, but the fact is that most are just in search of a story. This is the case with programmes like *Your Call*. Its purpose is simply to create entertaining radio, an end it achieves through orchestrating conflict – moreover, conflict in which there is no attempt at resolution. Nobody ever wins one of these debates.

Another episode concerned the tragic case of John Hogan who, while suffering from clinical depression, plunged from a hotel balcony in Crete with his two children, killing one of them in the process. Hogan was tried before a judge and jury in Greece and acquitted of murder. In his summing up, the judge accepted that Hogan was suffering from mental illness at the time of the tragedy, and said that living with the consequences of his actions was punishment enough. Enough for the judge and for John Hogan perhaps, but not, it turns out, enough for *Your Call* which wants to give its listeners the chance to Have Your Say. And of course they do. Considering none of the evidence, callers ring in to make various points with equally unfounded conviction. Thus we learn that 'a life is a life', that the judge is 'an absolute disgrace', and we are asked to consider 'the poor mother'. After listening for some time things take a surreal turn as people start to build upon uninformed comments made by previous callers: 'I don't know anything about this case, but I just want to pick up on a point one of the other callers made earlier...'

We have become used to the modern style of interviewing that is confrontational and aggressive. Broadcast journalists in particular no longer show any deference to their interviewees. They tend to be aggressive by default and forensic in their execution. Jeremy Paxman, presenter of BBC's flagship current affairs programme *Newsnight*, is perhaps the most famous exponent of this kind of political interview. He admitted that his motivation during an interrogation is to discover, 'Why is this lying bastard lying to me?'

In the hands of a journalist as skilled as Paxman, the gladiatorial nature of this kind of investigation can be revealing and entertaining, but not always. Media training ensures that politicians and interviewees from bigger corporations and organisations do not enter the arena unprepared or unarmed.

It is fairly easy to identify a subject who has been well trained and briefed. The three golden rules of media training are: to know what you are going to say and keep saying it; to never explore the hypothetical or the theoretical; and finally, never to refuse or decline to comment, but instead use a bridging statement to link to the subject you really want to talk about. For example, say you attend an interview with a really good anecdote about your father that you'd like to tell, but the interviewer asks you, 'How is your mother?' You would respond by saying, 'She's really busy at the moment, looking after my father who is...' and then break into your pre-prepared story.

If an interviewee does attempt to answer a hypothetical 'What if...?' question, the only thing they can be certain of is that they will be wrong, and the only moot point is how wrong they are going to be. In attempting to answer questions of this type, the best that they can hope to achieve is to give the interviewer a big stick to hit them with at some later date. No one wants to make an 'on the record' statement which will be used against them in the future, and that is why well-briefed people don't answer these questions. Instead you'll hear them use phrases such as 'I think the real issue is…', 'The important thing to remember is…', 'I think the bigger question is…'. These can be heard on air hundreds of times every day.

What we have ended up with is a war of attrition in which the truth is an early casualty. The interviewees' priority is to get through the interview without saying anything incriminating. The media likes to blame PRs for this, but they themselves are just as complicit. You can see from the case of Ainsworth that his willingness to speculate on a possible solution was seized upon by the media as an example of weakness and woolly thinking. Rather than view his openness and candour as refreshing, he was accused of not having 'thought things through' and was demonised for it. My first advice to anyone looking to raise their profile through PR is always: if you can't think of a really good reason to speak to the media, then don't.

The same is true whoever you are. Interviews with members of the public, who have not had the benefit of media training and are unused to the techniques of the modern interviewer, can in theory provide a refreshingly open alternative to those with a briefed adversary. That is certainly a big part of their appeal to editors and researchers. Yet it is more often the case that these people are subjected to the same kind of forensic questioning. Where Paxman leads the less able follow, and many of those conducting interviews in the same confrontational style often sound at best patronising (see Nicky Campbell), but more often the interviewee is simply being bullied or being made to look stupid.

On 13 December 2010, BBC News Channel broadcast an interview with Jody McIntyre, a disabled man who was taking part in a demonstration against the introduction of tuition fees, when he was pulled from his wheelchair and dragged across the road by the police. The entire incident was caught on film and posted on YouTube. Adopting his natural gladiatorial stance, journalist Ben Brown prefaced the interview by providing a voiceover to the film, which showed police pulling McIntyre out of his wheelchair and dragging him across the road to the pavement. However Brown's commentary was much more equivocal than the images: 'These pictures appear to show police pulling Jody McIntyre – political activist and blogger – out of his wheelchair and dragging him across the road to the pavement.' Brown went on to suggest that McIntyre might have caused the situation to occur by 'wheeling himself towards the police'. When this inflammatory line of enquiry quickly proves fruitless, Brown states that he himself had seen protestors throwing rocks at police and asks if McIntyre was throwing anything.

At no point prior to this has there been any suggestion that McIntyre has thrown anything, moreover this is a man obviously suffering from cerebral palsy, incapable of 'wheeling himself' anywhere, let alone gathering rocks and hurling them at people. Ultimately, McIntyre proves more than a match for Brown, articulately stating that this incident involving himself is a distraction, stirred up by the media to draw attention away from the main issue, which is the education cuts. I'm not sure whether that's true, but it's an interesting position and surely worthy of investigation; indeed one might expect a journalist of Brown's training and calibre to pick up on that. Instead he asks McIntyre again whether he threw anything or 'shouted anything provocative' to incite the police. McIntyre sums the exchange up perfectly by describing Brown's questions as 'ludicrous'.

The interview led to a mountain of complaints, partly due to an Internet campaign which resulted in the incident reaching a much wider audience. In response, Kevin Bakhurst, controller of the BBC News Channel, defended Ben Brown by saying: 'We interviewed Mr McIntyre in the same way that we would have questioned any other interviewee in the same circumstances.' That much, at least, is true. Not all interviewees are as articulate as McIntyre and not all incidents of bullying as blatant as Brown's, but whether you're Mick from Cleckheaton or Nick Clegg, if you speak to the media, you should expect whatever you say to come under intense, and probably uncomfortable, scrutiny.

The irony is that, despite our high level of ignorance, the market for our opinion has never been greater. How fortunate, then, that ignorance is no barrier to holding opinions. We are happy to offer them about everything: 'The subject of today's phone-in: Quantum Physics. Is the search for the Higgs boson a waste of taxpayers' money or is it the key to understanding life, the universe and everything? Call us now and Have Your Say…'

Relying on the opinion of people who literally don't know what they are talking about is dangerous, but one group's voice is never heard. Whatever the subject, we will never hear the voice of the equivocal majority. When asked for their views of the popular talent show *The X Factor*, *Your Call*'s listeners were either vitriolic in their hatred, or passionate in their support. I don't really watch *The X Factor*. I have seen a few episodes, because my wife and daughters are big fans, but it does nothing for me. I don't like the show – people I've never heard of singing songs I never wanted to hear again – but I don't hate it particularly, nor do I think Simon Cowell is killing music. I don't feel something more worthy should be shown in its place, in fact I don't think I've watched any programme on ITV in that time slot for the best part of 30 years. In this respect, I'm like almost every one of my friends. I've never had a conversation with anyone about *The X Factor*; I couldn't tell you who the winners are, let alone the contestants. Consequently I could never ring in to a radio show, write a blog or post a comment on Facebook in order to Have My Say. I suspect there are a great many people who share this view, but the process of being constantly invited to Have Your Say on every issue, whilst listening to others have theirs, makes it increasingly difficult to maintain an open mind or say you have no opinion, or that you simply don't care.

The demand for User Generated Content is vast, but in reality nobody cares what happens as a result of Having Your Say at all. Our lives and opinions have become reduced to content: dramas in which we play a starring part, and there have never been more roles available.

Chapter 12
Making Friends and Influencing People

'While it is true that the best advertising is word of mouth, never lose sight of the fact that it can also be the worst advertising.' – *Dr Jef I. Richards, Professor of Advertising, University of Texas*

For companies looking to launch a new product – which is to say, almost all of them – Everything Now appears to provide the perfect environment. Consumers, like a nest full of baby birds, sit with mouths open wide in eager anticipation of whatever titbit might come their way. There is no question of *need* – the conceptual nature of the economy means that these birds will carry on eating, even when they are fuller than foie gras geese – but a question of *want*. However, this doesn't mean that launching a new product is easy. Taking a product to market is very difficult and enormously expensive. Despite the fact that brands are consummate professionals at communication, only one in five product launches ends in success. The fact is that these birds can sing.

Marketers and psychologists have long understood the process by which new ideas, or innovative products, move through a population or social network. Facebook, LinkedIn, Twitter and all the other channels by which information can be exchanged are new phenomena, but the underlying process determining how this information will be exchanged remains the same.

In 1962, research sociologist Everett Rogers originated the *Theory of the Diffusion of Innovations*. Rogers proposed that a small proportion of the population typically adopts new products, or ideas, before they achieve broad acceptance or mass-market appeal.

What is more, it is this group's willingness to adopt an innovation, based on awareness, interest, evaluation and trial, that ultimately determines how successful the product will be with the majority of the market. Rogers called this group the Early Adopters but they are also known as Opinion Formers, Taste Makers or Trendsetters.

Early Adopters are significant for two reasons. Firstly, they are the first group of customers to purchase a new product. They might be your most loyal fans, who can provide valuable feedback about how a new product performs in the field, or they may be completely new customers who are simply after the cachet of being first. They might be the kind of people who have a games console, smartphone, 3D TV or Blue-ray DVD player as soon as they became available; they might be among the first to try out a new gym when it opens; or the ones to invest in a solar heating system or a hybrid car before anyone else. They might be the people who need to see a movie on the opening night, or those who subscribe to a specialist magazine to ensure they're up with all the latest news.

Early Adopters are exceptional, but not rare, constituting around 13.5 percent of the population. We all know someone who is an Early Adopter – indeed you may have been one, for at least some of the time. People can fall into different categories for different innovations: a car fanatic might be an Early Adopter of new sports cars, but a Late Majority Adopter of technology.

The second reason that Early Adopters are important to the marketers and brands is, not only do they buy things first, but also they tell the rest of us all about them. This process is called 'word of mouth' and stimulating it is the goal of everyone involved in the launch of a new product. In fact, word of mouth is so important, it is arguably the only thing they need to consider. A product might not necessarily succeed as a result of good word of mouth, but without it, failure is as good as guaranteed.

This is because most of us, the 68 percent that makes up the Early Majority and Late Majority (to use Rogers' terms) rely heavily upon the endorsement of Early Adopters to inform our buying decisions. Most of us don't subscribe to specialist magazines or read product reviews and we don't need to see a film, read a book or play a game the instant it comes out and we are happy to get into a 'new band' as soon as they've completed their fourth album. If we're thinking of buying a flat screen TV, we are most likely to ask our friend Robert – who bought one as soon as they were introduced – which model he recommends we should go for. For movies, TV shows and games, word of mouth can make or break a title, within days of launch. The success of the film *Paranormal Behaviour*, Elbow's Mercury Award-winning album *The Seldom Seen Kid* and Rovio's *Angry Birds* mobile phone game, was due to word of mouth. In each of these cases, marketing spend was limited. Conversely, despite millions of dollars' worth of advertising support, the lack of word of mouth killed heavily marketed properties like Bruce Willis's *Red*, Guns N' Roses' *Chinese Democracy* and Square Enix's *Final Fantasy XIV*.

Brands try to stimulate word of mouth by providing us with what they call 'social currency'. Social currency is information which we can share with other people that encourages further social encounters. For football fans social currency may be provided by knowledge of the transfer market or an opinion on the impending fortunes of a manager, player or club; for somebody interested in fashion it may involve knowing what the colours of the season are going to be or how to 'get the look' of a voguish celebrity. Social currency can increase an individual's sense of self-worth, providing status and recognition, but more likely, it simply allows one to engage in interaction with colleagues, acquaintances and friends, building a community by establishing common ground.

Young people feel a particular pressure to accrue and dispense social currency in order to engage with their peers. As a teenager, I can remember how esoteric knowledge about music trends, gained through sedulous patronage of John Peel and the *NME*, could result in brief, but deeply satisfying alpha-male status within my own circle of friends. Unfortunately, the girls we were secretly trying to impress were much more interested in soap operas, clothes and the Top 40, thereby demonstrating that social currency, outside of its peculiar social network, can often have a very poor exchange rate.

Social currency also creates an affiliation between brands and their customers. It increases consumer engagement and provides them with enough information and knowledge to have a conversation around the brand. Consumers get a feeling of belonging and an opportunity to develop their own identity within their peer group.

It's much easier to see how this works in practice. Let's say you are looking for a pair of trainers. One pair of trainers is much the same as another, but we have seen that simply adding a brand – like Nike or Adidas – can affect our attitude to essentially identical products. For some, selecting a pair of trainers may simply be an issue of style and comfort, but for many many more, these issues pale into insignificance against the challenge of buying the right or – God forbid – the wrong trainers.

This challenge could be addressed by assiduously reading style magazines or websites, but a much easier way, and therefore much more common, is to ask the opinion of family, friends or peers. If this information proves to be sound, and the style police are appeased, then the value of the information and respect for the person who provided it will increase. The new purchaser may even turn into another advocate for the brand, passing on their good opinion of the trainers to others, and the cycle will continue.

The popularity of social networks like Facebook and Twitter have given this process much more structure and, from the marketer's point of view, this has made it much more effective. It is an opportunity that brands have been keen to exploit, in the spirit of the old adman's adage, to 'go fishing where the fish are'. At the time of writing, Facebook has 500 million users worldwide and is growing at a rate of 400,000 new users per day. Display and TV adverts now direct viewers to the product's Facebook page rather than to some unloved corporate website. During the 2010 World Cup, Adidas conducted virtually all its marketing activity through online channels.

But using these social networks as a marketing channel is not without its dangers. Firstly, on the web, having your say is all pervasive, but the freedom to publish whatever you want is also the freedom to publish whatever you want. Here, what's sauce for the Dawkins Goose is sauce for the McKeith Gander: experts and idiots alike find it equally easy to get their ideas, or even the lack of them, across and so naysayers will be able to spread their damning, reprehensible opinion of your fantastic new product with just the same expediency as your most ardent fans. It can be very difficult for observers to distinguish the reliability of the source, because poorly researched nonsense and insightful critique looks much the same when it's on the page and only 140 characters long. Secondly, despite the obvious benefits of some kind of filtering mechanism, the egalitarian nature of the social networks means that there can be no quality control. If we applied the Project Triangle to content generated by users of Facebook or Twitter, then I expect we'd be likely to find 99.9 percent pushing at the quality and cost angles, but thereby gaining from the ability to be delivered almost instantly. Finally, Nick Davies is right about the influence of public relations on the media, but he misses the point. As far as the PRs are concerned, the media has never been an end in itself, merely a means to one. PRs view media outlets as channels that can take their message through to the target audience: undeniably useful, but also difficult to manage. There isn't a PR in the world that wouldn't rather just miss them out altogether, and UGC gives them the opportunity to do just that.

The traditional mass media – national newspapers, TV channels, radio stations – deliver huge audiences to their advertisers, but depending upon what product you are promoting, the vast proportion of this audience is irrelevant to you. Say, for example, you secured a review for your new mobile phone model in the *InGear* section of the *Sunday Times* (which covers cars and technology). The *Sunday Times* sells around 1.2 million copies each week, but we have seen that it contains quite a lot of information – around 36 hours' worth. Most people breeze through this in about 45 minutes, which means that your article only has a chance of being seen by the subgroup who reads the *InGear* section. Even then, only a proportion of that section's readers will browse the mobile phone reviews page that week. Furthermore, it will only be relevant to the people in this group who are also in the market for a new mobile phone. I don't know how many people that is, but I expect that it's a tiny proportion of the original figure of 1.2 million. It helps to think of this process as a funnel, with a huge number of people going into the top, but just a trickle of people – the ones you've reached – coming out of the bottom.

Online, things work in precisely the reverse. There are no massed audiences here. Every person's experience of the web is unique, but because we are all connected and exchanging information, the potential audience is massive. Only 1 percent of people online create content; a further 10 percent distribute it while the remaining 89 percent consume it. The key to marketing success in this environment is to get the 1 percent to start talking about your story and encourage the 10 percent to start distributing it through links and comments. This is viral marketing and it works by relying on the fact that the people doing the distribution will know enough about the likes and dislikes of the others in their network to only refer on items that will be relevant.

As we interact with people in our own network, we quickly learn that those links Paul posts on our Facebook wall are usually worth clicking on, so we encourage Paul to keep up the good work by clicking the thumbs up button to show him we like them. In a similar way, our own online activity allows web brands like Facebook to gather metadata about what we like and what we don't like, which in turn allows them to serve us adverts or provide us with links to products and services that we are likely to find engaging. As far as brands are concerned, this is the equivalent of a guarantee that your advert or PR will only be seen by members of your target audience. Returning to our previous example, it's like guaranteeing that everyone who reads the *Sunday Times* and is thinking of buying a mobile phone will read your review or see your ad. For the brands, this is a compelling proposition, but with so much information and so many messages trying to reach us, the temptation is to go even further, because the most persuasive form of advertising is the kind that doesn't look like advertising at all.

The fastest growing areas of PR and marketing are all digital. Companies spend a fortune on an activity known as search engine optimisation (SEO), which is nothing more nor less than an attempt to fool the users of search engines like Google that a website is more popular than it really is. When you type a word or phrase into Google, you're often met with many pages of results. Google ranks the list in what it thinks is the most appropriate order, using information it has gathered about the websites themselves, most important of which is how many web pages are linked back to them. So if you type in 'McKevitt' to Google, you might discover around 126,000 links. The most popular of these, which is the one ranked first, is a Wikipedia entry for Michael McKevitt, the leader of the terrorist paramilitary organisation known as 'The Real IRA' (whom, I feel I must stress, is no relation). Down the page in seventh place is a link to my LinkedIn home page. If I wanted to be the top McKevitt, I could hire a firm of SEO marketers who are expert in how search engines work and what people search for. They would employ a host of tactics to improve my popularity, from editing the content on my site, thereby making Google think it is more relevant, to generating a host of bland online articles every day, each one linking back to my site from other sites, which would make Google believe that I am more popular than I really am. Obviously, when the term is 'McKevitt', the competition is pretty weak, but when it's something like 'Home Insurance' or 'Hotels in London' there can be many organisations trying to do the same thing and that is when it starts to get really expensive.

The result is an invisible but tangible impact on how many people visit the website. The beauty of this process is that while it might be invisible to the customer, to a marketer commissioning the activity, like all marketing activity online, it is very easy to measure its effectiveness. You can gauge the success of a campaign simply by comparing your position in searches and comparing the number of click-throughs you get before your marketing campaign started then comparing that to the same activity during and after it has finished.

PRs are used to being invisible, so while the combination of anonymity, transparency and reach offered by the social network sites presents a tantalising raft of tactical options for getting the message across, the key benefit is that communication can be achieved without having to rely on those obdurate middlemen in the media. The challenge is no longer to persuade a journalist that your story is newsworthy and your position valid, but to engage the audience directly, while at the same time persuading them that your intentions are genuine and that your offer is benign. You might be surprised at just how willing people are to engage, but remember that for around 20 years we have been told that our opinion is important, so it should be of no surprise that the most successful campaigns are the ones that invite consumers, whether implicitly or explicitly, to have their say.

In December 2009, an Essex couple, Tracy and Jon Mortimer, started a Facebook campaign to make the song 'Killing in the Name' by Rage Against the Machine, the UK Christmas Number One single. Their real aim was to keep that year's *X Factor* winner, Joe McElderry, off the top spot. The exercise was a resounding success and they persuaded half a million people to download the track in a single week. The couple's only motivation was that they were 'Fed up of Simon Cowell's latest karaoke act being Christmas Number One', but for PRs and marketers, it was a demonstration of how effective – and cheap – a well-orchestrated social network campaign can be, especially when it taps into the zeitgeist.

There have been many attempts to repeat the Mortimers' success and the news pages of the marketing and PR trade press have been filled with stories announcing the launch of digital PR arms or stand-alone, digital PR agencies. What there has not been – yet – is any evidence that these professionals can produce a campaign with anywhere near as much impact. In fact, many of the following year's biggest stories involved online campaigns that went horribly wrong, because while the web is good at spreading news, it doesn't care whether it's good or bad.

In March 2010, Nestlé was forced to respond to a barrage of criticism concerning its response to a YouTube campaign run by Greenpeace that highlighted the alleged environmental impact of its palm oil plantations on rainforests in South America and South East Asia. Nestlé found itself in a position not only of having to rebut these claims, but also of defending its handling of the subsequent furore, played out across social media networks. First off, Nestlé demanded that the Greenpeace video be removed from YouTube. This only served to drive tens of thousands of viewers to seek out the video, curious to find out what all the fuss was about, which in turn provided further fuel for the blogging engine. Things took a turn for the worse when an anonymous moderator from Nestlé started arguing with posters on the company's official Facebook page. This led to a flurry of complaints that his insensitive comments were irreverent, rude and disrespectful to consumers who wanted to raise genuine concerns about the environmental impact of Nestlé's business activities.

The coup de grâce, however, was a further online ad campaign run by Greenpeace, which used the same SEO criteria as Nestlé. This meant that whenever people typed a key search term into Google – like 'Nestle', 'Kit-Kat', 'Have a break', 'Greenpeace' or even 'Chocolate' – they were immediately shown an ad that proclaimed, 'Have a Break - Which chocolate company destroys rainforests for palm oil?' and contained a link to Greenpeace's own website.

Online PR can be very powerful, but with great power comes great responsibility. Within social networks, there is an issue of permission that doesn't exist in traditional media. Sites like Facebook are cosy environments for their users, places they can share information and interact with family and friends. Imagine it's Friday night and you're at a restaurant, enjoying dinner with a group of close friends. The evening is going well. You're on top form and your fellow diners are eagerly anticipating the denouement to another of your hilarious anecdotes. Then, just as you're about to deliver the punchline, a complete stranger appears at the table and rudely interrupts the conversation. He introduces himself as Colin and asks if any of you would like to test drive the new Nissan Micra. I'm guessing your reaction in this situation would be entirely negative. I mean, who the hell does this Colin think he is? Perhaps you'd go so far as to tell him exactly where he can stick his free test drive. You might invite all your friends to give the rude man equally short shrift. And who could blame you if you did?

A far-fetched scenario until you swap the restaurant for Facebook, because this is what happens when digital PR is done badly, as it is most of the time. In the olden days, bad PR – the sort that no one admitted to practising, but the one that, at the same time, seemed very familiar to journalists – consisted of emailing an announcement to scores of media contacts no matter how irrelevant it might be, waiting for a few hours, then systematically ringing every one of them up and asking a) whether they had received your press release and b) whether they planned to use it.

No journalist is ever interested in announcements: what they want are stories. The majority of press releases contain nothing of interest, even to the people writing them. Journalists will receive hundreds of these – variations on the theme of 'Company Launches New Tent'. Less frequently they'll receive one that says, 'Company Sells 1,000,000 Tents', which is also an announcement. On very rare occasions, they'll receive one that says, 'Last year 2,500 babies were conceived inside a tent'. This is a story.

The PR's newfound ability to foist announcements directly on the end user doesn't make them interesting or welcome. For communication to take place, an emotional connection needs to be made. People measure their lives in terms of experiences accumulated rather than possessions: defining themselves by the things they've done rather than by the things they've acquired. Nowhere is this more evident than on the social network sites. Material goods, the former badges of success, have lost their cachet. The new measures of achievement are experiences, which are easily captured as words, pictures, audio or video, thanks to the marvels of digital media. These kinds of User Generated Content are intensely personal and of little interest to anyone other than the creators – the modern equivalent of an evening's trawl through the next-door neighbours' holiday slides – but once they have been shared with the whole wide world via the world wide web, they become something else: totems of lives less ordinary.

Online social networks may not charge you for making use of their services, but there is a cost involved. Some people really do believe that free is the new price of everything, but if you're one of them, you'll shortly be going out of business. Somebody always has to foot the bill, so although you might not be paying money to use Facebook, Google, Spotify or Twitter, you can rest assured that you are paying with something: information. If you're trying to launch your brand to an audience of consumers who are bombarded by over 3,000 messages a day, then you're going to have to do something out of the ordinary to get their attention.

Chapter 13
The Empathy Tango

'If there is any one secret of success, it lies in the ability to get the other person's point of view and see things from his angle as well as your own.' – *Henry Ford, founder the Ford Motor Company*

Today it was Customer Service Day at my branch of Bank of Scotland. I know this because my visit – or, if you will, 'customer experience' – was out of the ordinary. In fact, I'd go so far as to say that not only was it different to the other 300 or so visits I've made, but it was also the singular occasion when it was different in any respect at all.

Until today, my weekly visits to the bank – exclusively to pay cheques in to our business bank account – had been a textbook study in pleasant, unexceptional routine. This is a business branch, so although it's in the city centre, there is rarely a queue and I'm usually in and out in less than five minutes. The usual drill goes like this:

I press the button next to the front door to request access. The cashier buzzes me in to the bank. I walk up to the counter and, with a smile, I hand over my paying-in book and the cheques, asking, 'Can I pay these in please?'

The cashier, who is always a female, smiles back and replies, 'Of course.'

She checks the amounts, stamps the paying-in book and passes it back to me with another smile. We both say thank you – that curiously English affectation – and I leave.

That is pretty much all there has ever been to report (save for the time a man came in looking for the Royal Bank of Scotland by mistake – my, how we laughed!). It's not a disagreeable chore and the cashiers are always polite, friendly, efficient and smiley, so while it's hardly the visceral thrill offered by, say, *The Guardian* Quick Crossword, I've no complaints about either the experience or the service. I've never given it much thought before, but I'd confidently say that you'd be hard-pushed to improve on it. Which is why today's events came as such a surprise.

I press the button next to the front door to request access. The cashier buzzes me in to the bank. I walk up to the counter and, with a smile, I hand over my paying-in book and the cheques, asking, 'Can I pay these in please?'

The cashier smiles back and replies, 'Of course.'

She checks the amounts, stamps the paying-in book and passes it back to me with another smile. And says, 'Would you like a cup of coffee?'

Before I have time to assimilate this non sequitur, she reaches down below the counter and produces a massive tin of Cadbury's Roses, 'Or one of these?'

Now I feel not just confused but awkward; like a 14-year-old on a first date. I've never been offered coffee in a bank before. And to make things worse, this is the pretty cashier – the one with the interesting glasses. Maybe I should say yes. I've just had a coffee, but I don't want to offend her. We've got on so well over the years; it would be a shame to ruin it all with a clumsy faux pas. It might be instant coffee. I don't really like instant coffee. Enquiring about the quality of the coffee on offer might make me look like a bit of a snob or even ungrateful. Would it be rude to have the coffee, but to take it outside? Or does saying yes mean that I'll have to drink it here, perhaps making small talk? All I've ever said to her is, 'Can I pay this in please?' and 'Thank you'. To be honest, I've never really felt the need to take our relationship to the next level. What would we talk about anyway? She must be almost half my age. Would she be interested in seeing a picture of my kids? Or maybe she has work to do and doesn't want to talk at all. I'll have to stand here, drinking superheated instant coffee that I don't want, on my own in the foyer of the bank, ignored by staff and smiling gauchely at other customers who wonder what I'm doing. And all the way through this sorry process, I'll be hoping that the world would swallow me whole until finally I'm able to leave with a blistered mouth, and the cashiers at this branch of Bank of Scotland will talk about that strange bloke who was just in.

All things considered, I decide to skip the coffee.

'That's very kind, but no thanks, I've just had a cappuccino,' I say, pointing my thumb over my shoulder in the direction of the tram stop. I decide it would be rude not to take a sweet. I really want two – one Cadbury's Rose is never enough I find – but I don't want to appear greedy.

Before I leave, I feel I'm owed an explanation, 'This is all a bit... unusual isn't it?' I ask, as I unwrap my caramel.

'It's Customer Service Day. Orders from Head Office,' she replies flatly.

What was the thinking that led me to endure this bizarre experience? Is it that Bank of Scotland is such an efficient, customer-focused organisation that, after months of discussion, research and deliberation, it realised the only possible way to improve its service was – for one day only – to offer cups of instant coffee and singular Cadbury's Roses to all of its business account holders who visited a branch? It's safe to assume that this is probably not the case.

The real explanation is slightly more complicated, but is worth exploring because it highlights not only how difficult it is for brands to cut through the noise of Everything Now and communicate effectively with customers, but also why we are all going to be experiencing a lot more initiatives like Customer Service Day in the future.

Taken in isolation, Customer Service Day does seem like a ludicrous initiative, but it will have made perfect sense to decision-makers who got behind the idea. To understand why, we need to first consider what it is that customers are looking for from their bank. Speaking as a long-standing business account holder, I'd say the list of qualities is not particularly long. Firstly, I'd like to know that my money is secure. Secondly, I'd like to have an account that is easy to manage: one I can pay in to and withdraw from without too much difficulty. Thirdly, I'd like there to be an account manager who is competent and efficient. It would be nice if they at least feigned interest in my business from time to time, but I'd settle happily for someone who was simply capable and polite. Finally, if it comes to raising money or difficult trading times, I'd like helpful advice and as much support as possible.

I believe that this list covers just about everything a small business needs or wants. It is not meant to be a revelation – every bank knows what its customers expect from it – but more an illustration of how easy this information is to discover. There are no expensive research projects required here. Against this criteria, I'd score Bank of Scotland at about 6 out of 10: not good enough for me to ever recommend them to anyone else, but not bad enough for me to ever think about moving the account to another bank either.

Suffice to say, Customer Service Day doesn't enter into consideration, making not one iota of difference to the score. Looking back through the correspondence I've received from Bank of Scotland over the past eight years, I can see that, in all that time, it has never once introduced a service that I've felt anything more than ambivalent about. Its website is okay, a bit clunky, but I've learned to work around several of the most annoying idiosyncrasies, so overall the online service can be regarded as adequate. There was one occasion when I asked our account manager whether she thought it might be useful for the business to have an overdraft facility, but she pretty much killed the conversation stone dead by immediately making it clear they wouldn't sanction 'any borrowing at all under any circumstances' and hoped I would understand that (I did), but then we didn't need the overdraft in any case, so her position caused us few problems. In Bank of Scotland's defence, none of the other banks, many of whom send us expensive-looking items of direct mail on at least a bi-monthly basis, has been able to convince us that our business's financial needs would be any better served under their aegis.

No one I know ever talks about their bank with any great enthusiasm and, certainly, I have yet to meet anyone who's so delighted with the service they're getting that they've taken it upon themselves to tell me about it. I used to imagine that you'd be more satisfied if you were a big corporate customer, but having formerly been a director of a plc, during both good and bad times, my experience was that the service was fine when things were going well, but the moment the going got tough, then so did the bank.

If the customer requirement is so clear, the question is why aren't any of the banks performing better than adequately? One reason is that there is a lot of customer inertia within the banking sector. Banks are a bit like toilet paper, performing an essential service adequately well, but not something you customers are going to get excited about, and so they're only likely to change supplier if something goes wrong. Outside of the marketing bumf and advertising, in the real world, you rarely hear people or businesses talking about how great their bank is, but very few people move their accounts around, tending to stick with whichever they signed up for in the first place through thick and thin.

This doesn't explain why all the banks engage initiatives like Customer Service Day. And I do mean all, because this sort of activity is not peculiar to Bank of Scotland. Walking past the branch of Barclays in the city centre, I noticed a poster featuring a photo of the team (who presumably all work within it) and the slogan, 'Our mums think we are the best bankers in the world'. Now, I love my mum too, but when it comes to corporate finance, while she's not the last person in the world I'd go to for advice, she's certainly some way off being the first. The notion, then, that

I should care what the mothers of some persons unknown to me think of their financial expertise would be laughable, but for the banking crisis of 2008, which makes me think that said mothers might have made a better job of it. As with Customer Service Day, this kind of activity looks ad hoc and homey, but branches have very little control over their own communications, so it was certainly the result of some central marketing strategy, intended to make the company seem less intimidating and more personable.

The same can be said for the national advertising campaigns. Whether it's Lloyds TSB with their cutesy, animated characters living in a green and pleasant land or, perhaps most notably, Halifax's long-running homespun series 'starring' ordinary members of staff, the aim is to engage our sensibilities rather than our good sense. That is why Halifax treats us to songs – like Trevor from the Leeds branch singing 'Something Tells Me I'm Into Something Good' – and sketches – like the unforgettable 'ISA ISA Baby' in which the team pretends to run the company radio station with the same ruthless efficiency that they no doubt used to run the mortgage department circa 2007, achieving equally hilarious results – rather than to facts and figures. The challenge for banks is that while they can all claim to provide us with everything we need adequately well, they can offer us nothing that is unique. And even if one did start to offer a unique service, it would almost certainly become ruinously expensive to do so and all the others would simply copy them anyway.[6]

Banks do try to differentiate themselves by giving us things that we might want, like cheaper loans or higher interest rates on savings, but even here, given that they're all operating identical business models and selling the same thing – money – there's not much more that they can do but twiddle at the margins. For example, Bank A could offer borrowers a lower initial rate of interest than anyone else, but they would need to tie their customers into a

[6] See the Credit Crunch of 2008.

longer term with greater early settlement penalties than the rest. In the event, none of this is enough to make most of us choose Bank A over Bank B, because another problem is that people don't shop around. There is a tendency to treat banks like supermarkets, buying all one's financial services from the same place, regardless of value. What we end up with then is the same illusion of choice we found in the soap or toothpaste sector. Superficially we have hundreds of different loans, mortgages, ISAs and savings accounts to choose from, but beneath the surface, they are identical products packaged in slightly different ways, which means a rational, evidence-based decision requires enormous effort.

This is why, despite all the advice to look at everything on offer, most first-time homebuyers just walk into the local branch of their bank or building society and ask for a mortgage. For the banks, the upside of this inertia is clear: once you've attracted a new customer, there's a good chance that you'll be able to provide them with a lifetime's worth of financial services. The downside is that persuading them to choose you in the first place is not easy. The rewards for success are great, but the failure rate is high.

The same is true for most categories, not just banking. In the past, companies sold us products and services by identifying a need and then matching the benefits of whatever they were trying to sell to that need, developing what was called a value proposition. A value proposition is fine if your audience is making rational decisions, but less effective if they are guided by their emotions. In principle it should be easy to sell the benefits of a banana to someone who needs a snack, but if what they want is a doughnut, you've got no chance of succeeding.

Today, empathy is what you need to succeed, not a value proposition. The products and services that are most successful today are the ones that engage our sympathies; they are the ones that appear to empathise with us. If a brand can show it cares about its customers, it can create something that connects with them. This is what initiatives like Customer Service Day are all about.

What the bank is trying to do is to connect with us, not on a rational level on the basis of service values and product benefits, but on an emotional level, based on experience. Connecting with us in this way is what brands like Nike, Apple and Coca-Cola do so effectively and when something works, other people tend to copy it. The banks are trying to create a brand that we will empathise with; in simple terms, they are trying to get us to like them.

Customer Service Day epitomises the current trend for creating brands that have a more sympathetic corporate image. In the past, banks were seen as cold, remote institutions. Their advertising might have made out that they liked to say yes, or that they were a listening bank, but this was slightly at odds with the experience, in which they tended to do neither. The bank manager stereotype was always male: a pinstriped, upstanding member of the community and possibly a keen Rotarian. He was certainly not somebody you were ever going to be on first-name terms with, nor the sort of person who'd rush to tell you what his mum thought about his performance in the job.

Times have changed, and to succeed at all, today's corporations must give the impression that each individual customer matters to them. The trick is to give the impression that you are talking exclusively to one person, but do this to thousands of other people, if not millions, at the same time. One of the best examples of this cosy capitalism is Innocent Drinks. Formed in 1999, Innocent is famous for its wholesome, but bright and breezy 'Isn't it great to be alive?' philosophy, which is driven through its products' packaging and advertising ('containing: bananas, oranges and semi quavers and free from: additives, preservatives and gramophones', as it says on the carton). Innocent seems like a free-and-easy venture and indeed the whole story about its inception has been played and replayed many times over. At the turn of the century, three chums, who were great at making fruit smoothies, decided to test out the popularity of their delicious recipes at a local music festival. They invited customers to sample their wares free of charge and, in return, asked them to vote whether or not they felt that the trio should pack in their day jobs and start a proper business by placing the empty bottles in one of two bins marked 'Yes' and 'No'. Legend has it that the response to the question was an overwhelming 'Yes', with just one bottle in the 'No' bin. The rest is history.

It's a good story, but that's probably all it is. The reality is a little more contrived, but no less impressive. The three chums were all Cambridge graduates, with blue-chip backgrounds in marketing and advertising. They spent six months researching drinks recipes after identifying a gap in the chilled drinks market that was being ignored by the leading beverage manufacturers like Coca-Cola and Pepsi. Together with a multi-award winning design agency, they developed a brand that tapped not only into the zeitgeist for companies with a wacky, yet inclusive tone of voice (a legacy of the dotcom era) but also addressed environmental and nutritional concerns that were becoming prevalent.

Developing a product that met that brief was relatively straightforward: developing an iconic empathetic brand was the real achievement. Innocent started not with a great product idea, but with a great understanding of the market requirement. The team knew how to build a brand that could engage this audience. Customers connected not with the fruit-based product – I'm no gourmand, but I expect one carton of liquidised banana, orange and mango tastes much the same as the next to most people – but with the Innocent brand, which seemed to share their values and concerns in a way that Tropicana or Minute Maid, who dominated the fruit juice category at the time, just didn't.

Innocent didn't just feel like it was made especially for you, but that it cared especially for you as well. It was a brand that implicitly seemed to combine your concerns for the environment with your desire for a healthier lifestyle; that understood that you were unwilling to compromise on either taste or quality; and that recognised you wanted to have some fun along the way. Innocent has continued to make people feel like this even after it sold a major stake in its business to Coca-Cola for around £30 million in April 2009.[7]

The most successful brands all work in the same way. Apple can create an emotional desire for a phone or a computer that overpowers a rational understanding that an alternative device might be better. Aston Martin can create an emotional desire for a car that everybody wants, nobody needs and few can afford, yet still be perceived as understated when compared to its competitors Porsche, Ferrari or Lamborghini. Adidas can create an emotional desire for high-performance football boots and trainers that will make almost no difference to the actual performance of their wearer. For the banks, the key thing to learn from all this is that they should no longer spend their time trying to make their product different (which Everything Now is making increasingly difficult) and that their energy, time and money will be much better spent by making their brand different instead.

This is an easy principle to grasp, but alas one that proves much more difficult to achieve in practice. Knowing what needs to be done is not the same as knowing how to do it. Trying to make your brand stand out from the crowd is no pushover, which is why most business ventures end in failure. In the face of a potentially overwhelming amount of information, people have become expert at filtering out anything they don't consider relevant. You might have the best proposition in the world, but if you can't cut through that noise and make a connection with people, then you're as good as dead. Successful brands are built from the inside out: that means product and innovation are what drives the brand, not the other way round. Some companies call this approach 'Living the Brand' and it involves having a set of values – like being the friendliest, the wisest or the funniest – and trying to live them out through everything you do from innovative product development to communication with the customer. For

[7] Reported variously to be between 10 and 20 percent.

companies like Apple, Nike, Sony or Pepsi, who do this thing well, what we the consumers see in the advertising, packaging and products is just the tip of the iceberg, but if we were to look deeper, we'd find that the same company's values and messaging would be consistent at every contact point: whether that's an advert, speaking to someone in customer services, making a complaint, or seeing an interview with the CEO.

When something happens that's inconsistent with this brand image, customers can react very negatively, as Gerald Ratner found to his cost. On 23 April 1991, as the eponymous CEO of a hugely profitable high-street jewellery business, Ratner was invited to share the secret of his success in a speech to the Institute of Directors. Over 20 years later, it remains one of the finest examples of the value of branding over quality. His comments, arguably even more remarkable with hindsight, were widely reported at the time and almost caused the business to collapse, knocking £500 million off its share price. Ratner famously referred to the fact that his store sold a pair of earrings for just 99p, saying that while it was cheaper than a Marks and Spencer prawn sandwich it 'probably wouldn't last as long'. He went on to tell the audience, 'We also do cut-glass sherry decanters complete with six glasses on a silver-plated tray that your butler can serve you drinks on, all for £4.95. People say, "How can you sell this for such a low price?" I say, "Because it's total crap."' This is an extreme example, but consistency is the key if companies are to avoid 'doing a Ratner'.

Customer Service Day is what happens when the less adroit brands, who are inconsistent in their messaging, attempt at creating an empathetic link with the customer. The banks might know what to do, but they don't know how to do it. They see initiatives like this as the cherry on the cake, but forget that people don't buy the cherry – they buy the whole cake. Yes, handing out instant coffee and Cadbury's Roses, or telling people your mum thinks you're brilliant, might be different, but it's also irrelevant. Especially when, having been charmed by one of your lovely adverts with cutesy little people setting up home, or chuckling along with your invitation to open an ISA-ISA baby account, the customers who respond are told they need at least 25 percent deposit to get a mortgage and will receive just 2 percent in tax-free interest. More than this, I'd argue that what the banks are trying to achieve – getting everybody to like them – is to all intents and purposes impossible. Regardless, there's no shortage of advertising agencies queuing up to take their marketing millions and give it their best shot.

The uncomfortable space the banks find themselves in regularly requires them to make promises that they can't deliver. In 2010, NatWest ran a TV campaign to showcase its own vision to become 'Britain's Most Helpful Bank'. In the advert – which showed staff being helpful and happy customers being helped – the bank said it wanted to make: 'A public promise to become Britain's most helpful bank. It's why we created our customer charter. It's why, when you told us to open on Saturdays, we did. And why this year 160 branches will open earlier and close later.' Lovely stuff. Except it wasn't entirely true, as any customer making a visit to the 877 of its 1552 branches that remained closed on Saturday morning would have been able to attest. The advert was banned by the Advertising Standards Authority in December 2010 and NatWest forced to issue an apology.

In isolation, Customer Service Day seems ludicrous, because we can't step back and look at the activity of the banks as a whole. If we did, what we would see is a genuine attempt to build a brand which is friendly, approachable, here to serve you and which tries to manifest those qualities in every interface and communication with the public, but one that is doomed to fail, because the banks just can't deliver on these promises. In the past, banks competed with each other for customers on the basis of who could be seen as the friendliest, the most agreeable, the best listener, in other words, the one most likely to approve your overdraft, loan or mortgage application. It's no coincidence that, in 2008, the ones that said 'Yes' most often where also the ones who ended up in the deepest trouble.

The only thing that unites them all is the fact that they all had developed an idea for a product or service which they believed was going to fill a gap in the market. The reason that many of them failed is because they couldn't find an audience to connect with. Just because there is a gap in the market, it does not follow that there is a market in the gap.

The mergers in the finance sector post-2008 mean that there are fewer banks than ever before. Established names like Abbey and Bradford and Bingley were absorbed into other institutions and disappeared altogether. My own Bank of Scotland was reduced to the third part of an ugly acronym as part of Lloyds-HBoS. And here we arrive at another contradiction of Everything Now. Capitalism, whether cold-faced or cosy, is about creating competition. The purpose of a competition is to produce winners (and losers), not to provide choice, or even convenience. Indeed, one could argue that competition will lead to the eradication of choice, and this is certainly what we are witnessing in many categories, not just banking.

Even before the recession hit in 2008, every year 17 percent of businesses closed their doors. Statistically, only around half of start-ups will make it through their second year and just 20 percent will still be trading four years after they have launched. Business people don't like talking about failure, only success. In many companies I've worked with, words like 'problems' and 'threats' have been forbidden; they are called 'challenges' or 'opportunities' instead.

There are no recipes for success. You can read all the business books you like; the most you are likely to learn is how to write a case study. Serendipity plays a huge part in any success story, but it's usually written out of the book or the film. If it appears at all it's as a bit player. Typically, tomes offering entrepreneurial advice are written with 20:20 hindsight; a bit like being helicoptered onto the top of a mountain, and then working out how you might have gotten there if you'd climbed it. For the same reason, it's very difficult to learn anything from successful product or company launches. Large organisations are inherently inefficient, but admitting this doesn't go down well with the shareholders. Success is something shouted from the rooftops, failure something to be brushed under the carpet.

Yet without context, the successes are meaningless. I could provide you with a list of successful projects with which I have been involved, enough to make you think I have the Midas touch when it comes to business – it's the sort of thing we all do when we're applying for a job. But to do so would be disingenuous. I've been involved in my fair share of failures over the years and, despite my best efforts, I'm sure I will again in the future. Success in business might never have been more difficult to sustain than it is today, but serendipity has never been more important.

Chapter 14
'Yes! We Are All Individuals!'

'Most people are other people. Their thoughts are someone else's opinions, their lives a mimicry, their passions a quotation.' – *Oscar Wilde, playwright, author, poet*

Like the Chandler Bing character in *Friends*, I have real trouble explaining what I do for a living. It's not a big deal, but it can make small talk at parties a little awkward when the question emerges. I learned recently that I've got something called a 'Portfolio Career', which just means I do several different things. It's not a term I've found particularly helpful, making me sound either like I'm bragging or some kind of jack of all trades. Avoiding the question is not really an option either. It makes me look like I might do something shameful for a living – horse strangling perhaps – or that I am just being rude. I suppose I could provide a short list, but people don't really want that much information, and getting a two-minute monologue when all you expected was a one-word answer can be a bit dispiriting.

It's a very friendly thing to ask people what they do, it implies that you're interested in them. It is also very helpful because it means you can stereotype them, allowing you an additional mental tag especially if, like me, you're terrible at remembering names.

If I tell you someone you are going to meet is a doctor, nurse or physiotherapist, your expectations will be different than if I told you they were a corporate lawyer, investment banker or an accountant. Whether those expectations turn out to be correct really depends upon the individual, so it's important to remember that while stereotypes can be useful, they are not reality. Some stereotypes are great. When my wife tells people she's a consultant neurologist, people immediately think she must be super-bright and very caring (which she is). I usually tell people that, like the Chandler Bing character in *Friends*, I have real trouble explaining what I do for a living and immediately ask them a question about themselves in the hope that we can just leave it at that.

My problem is that I want to be seen as an individual, not a stereotype, which, ironically, is stereotypical of us all. We are at the centre of our own universe: a uniquely important, unique person. We naturally regard ourselves as a special case: individuals who are not one of the herd; one of those kids who is not like the others.

John Cleese tells a story about meeting a fan in 1978. He was in a hotel bar when a man he'd never met before introduced himself as one of the world's biggest Monty Python fans. The two started chatting, during which the fan revealed that his favourite part of the show was a recurrent joke about chartered accountants being very boring people. Cleese asked the fan what he did for a living.

'I'm an accountant,' he replied.

Cleese was surprised, and asked if the man was at all offended at these jokes being made at his profession's expense.

'Not at all,' the fan replied. 'You see, you make jokes about chartered accountants but I'm a certified accountant. They're completely different things.'

Cleese's conclusion was that the only way to convince someone that you are making a joke about them is to put their postcode at the bottom.

In Everything Now we are like the certified accountant: we feel like we are being treated as an individual but really we are being given the same things as everybody else. We express our individuality simply by choosing magnolia over vanilla or beige. The Project Triangle shows us that convenience is only possible if we sacrifice choice. We can buy any off-the-peg suit we like in the next 60 minutes, but no matter how much money we have to spend, a bespoke tailor will take several days to create one that is uniquely for us. The genius of Everything Now is that it provides the illusion of choice: there might be millions of things on offer, but behind the brand, under the bonnet or inside the packaging, it is all very similar.

Some time ago, I attended a party thrown by one of my wife's colleagues. Lots of doctors marry doctors. At this event, the neurological sciences were heavily represented, but there were also some anaesthetists, gynaecologists, oncologists, psychiatrists and even a few GPs. I was one of the few guests present without a medical background, but fortunately, what might have turned out to be a very long evening was saved by Toby, a friendly doctor I got talking to, who purported to share a common interest.

'Your wife tells me you're a big music fan, Steve. So am I.'

'Excellent,' I replied. 'Well, I suppose I am. What kind of music do you like?'

'Well, I don't like the usual, run-of-the-mill stuff,' Toby said intriguingly, 'I like things that are a little bit left-field; a little bit out there.'

'Interesting. Anyone I would have heard of?'

Toby thought for a moment and then started to count his favourite bands off against his fingers.

'Coldplay, The Stereophonics, Snow Patrol, Oasis and Keane.'

Three things struck me about this exchange. Firstly, had I been asked who the five biggest selling bands in the world that year were, I am confident that I would have rattled off an identical list to Toby's. Secondly, Toby's criteria for what constitutes 'left-field' is very different to my own: but that's not to scoff; it's my entirely subjective view. For a start, I am sure that all the bands on Toby's list, if questioned, would, just like the certified accountant, view themselves as 'a little bit different' to the others on the list. Thirdly, something or someone had managed to convince Toby, and literally millions of other people with identical music taste to his, that, in the face of overwhelming evidence, there was something esoteric about their love of melodic, middle-of-the-road, radio-friendly, rock music. This is the reason Everything Now works so brilliantly: while we are all unique individuals, it turns out that we all like pretty much the same things as everyone else.

Everything Now helps us celebrate our individuality by seeming to reach out to us and us alone – 'Because you're worth it', 'Because you deserve the best', 'Because you're special' – and then simply gives us all exactly the same thing as everybody else. That is why, as an expression of their individuality, millions of people buy the same Calvin Klein fragrances, Diesel jeans, Nike trainers, Burberry jackets and Coldplay CDs, thereby arriving at the same conclusion about themselves as Toby.

This is not some shocking truth, but it is a fact, and one that it is in no one's interests to acknowledge: the brands get to form a strong emotional bond with their target market, while we, the consumers, are made to feel special. It's easy to see why the brands do it, but explaining how they do it is a little more complicated. They are only able to do this at all because they know an awful lot about who we are and what we think, and they use this information, acquired at enormous expense, to make predictions about how we are likely to behave. Things don't always go to plan, after all many products fail, so they never make these predictions with total confidence. Consequently, they can never have too much information and will do all they can to harvest as much as possible.

In their publicity and advertising, all the major retailers talk about wanting to offer their customers choice. In reality, all they actually want is for everyone to buy everything from them. Choice, in this context, means nothing more than the opportunity for us to buy any item that they have elected to stock.

Tesco is the UK's leading retailer, and one of the world's biggest companies. It began by selling us groceries, but these days it sells us virtually everything – from fish fingers and furniture to finance and foreign holidays. This move into new markets, known as channel blurring, has been very successful. One in every seven pounds spent on the UK high street is spent at Tesco. As a result Tesco is now either the market leader or one of the market leaders in some surprising specialist categories. In music downloads, for example, Tesco Online accounts for ten percent of the total UK market, while in books it is number four in the sector, having seen off Borders, and behind only Waterstones, Amazon and WH Smith, with again, a ten percent share.

Tesco is no longer just a supermarket: it's a bank, insurance broker, mobile phone operator and music download platform. It's a place where you can book a vacation, get your home insurance or even exchange your old video games. It doesn't stop there. Retailers don't just want everybody to buy everything from them; what they want is, wherever possible, for you to buy their own brands. Their very nature puts them in a perfect position to get us to do this and the result, yet again, is less choice for the consumer.

So in a supermarket, while the range of goods and services across the board is vast, the choice within each category is usually extremely limited. Their size allows them to cherry-pick the biggest selling titles. Tesco might be the fourth biggest bookseller by volume, where it is possible to get the latest release by J. K. Rowling, Terry Pratchett or Jeremy Clarkson for a fraction of the cover price, but the number of different titles on offer will be tiny, more on a par with a motorway service station than a bookstore, and dwarfed by even the smallest branch of Waterstones. The same is true for music, games, films, clothes, homeware, magazines and a host of other categories. A high street newsagent – a typical branch of WH Smith or John Menzies perhaps – will carry about 4,500 different magazines each month. The average supermarket offers just 300 titles. You will probably be able to get a copy of the market-leading film magazine at your local Sainsbury, but you will find it more difficult to buy a copy of one of the others. Joanna Blythman, author of *Shopped*, offers this explanation:

> Supposedly supermarkets give us this fabulous choice and before supermarkets we were in this state of rationing. It's quite a psychological achievement

when you look at how narrow the choice really is. There is a choice, but it's not a qualitative choice. The real variety, the different crops that we used to grow have all gone. Very few people have challenged the supermarket idea that they provide choice.

Supermarkets don't put in any of the spade work either. You won't find Asda breaking many new authors or Waitrose supporting auteur DVD releases. And should Toby ever be tempted to push his music collection even further into the left-field, he will find the music section of Morrison's somewhat lacking in inspiration. The supermarkets' scale allows them to cream off the sales from their specialist competitors, so despite doing none of the tough grind, they enjoy the lion's share of the feast.

Supermarkets' promotion of own-label products has shifted competitive forces in favour of retailers. Not only do own brands make the highest contribution to gross margin, but they also drive customer loyalty and enhance the retailers' corporate reputation and brand image. Retailers have developed supply chain management systems of huge power and complexity, generating huge amounts of data on individual customers from point-of-sale scanners (EPOS data) and loyalty card schemes (over 80 percent of Tesco sales are made using the Club Card). They know more about your shopping habits than you do. Clearly this information provides them with a huge competitive advantage in terms of product research. They can easily identify which products are most popular with their customers and, thus, which own-label facsimiles are likely to prove the most successful. They are effectively de-risking their product development strategy. This gives them a massive advantage: approximately 85 percent of new FMCG products (things like packaged food, toiletries and household goods) spend less than 12 months on the supermarket shelves, so anything that can mitigate that degree of failure will have a huge impact on the bottom line.

Retail intelligence is a useful guide to our likes and dislikes, but it doesn't tell brands and retailers a great deal about us. For that kind of demographic information they can use something called Mosaic. Back in my undergraduate days, demographic profiling extended not much further than the socio-economic groups A, B, C1, C2 and D. These categories, which to be honest were never much use in the first place, have become increasingly weaker over time, thanks to the shift from a manufacturing to a service economy. We now have a proliferation of different worker grades and trends that this simple system was unable to take into account, like an increase in dual-income couples and the number of pensioners and students.

Mosaic is vastly more useful. It is a geodemographic tool owned by a company called Experian. It is used to classify residential postcode areas into distinct neighbourhoods, based on statistical information about the people who live there. Retail chains use the information to tailor stock to the needs of the local population while political parties and brands also use it to localise and finesse their national campaigns.

The beauty of Mosaic is that while our country contains well over 60 million people – each and every one of us a unique individual making our own contribution to life's rich tapestry – it manages to slot every single one of us into just 155 person types and 67 household categories. So you may think you're creatures of idiosyncratic habits and ideas (with left-field music tastes), perhaps even a little bit 'out there' (wherever 'there' might be), but in reality you're just like all the other New Urban Colonists, Corporate Chieftains and plain old Coronation Streets (although if you are the latter, then you are less likely to be reading this as your Mosaic profile tells me you're not really one for books).

Perhaps the best thing about Mosaic, though, is that it is multidimensional, so it picks up on subtleties. Some categories are concerned with job types – such as the aforementioned Corporate Chieftains – while others focus on housing (Coronation

Street, Dinky Developments), age (Stylish Single, Town Gown Transition), family structure (Middle-Rung Families), ethnicity (South Asian Industry) and whether the area is urban or rural. Mosaic can tell the brands and retailers things like what paper you're likely to read, what kind of holidays you like to go on, how often you watch ITV, what radio stations you listen to and even how likely you are to believe in a god (and which one). They can use this knowledge to work out how likely you are to buy their products.

Around 50 percent of the Mosaic data comes from the Census, with other sources including the edited electoral roll, Experian's credit database, house price data and government research. I don't know whether this says more about us or the marketers – that the whole of society can be boxed off effectively into just 155 categories – but for the brands, this knowledge is literally power: the power to sell us things. From that point of view, the Mosaic information is dynamite. Simply pull all the relevant information about your target categories and Bob's your Uncle (or rather he's your High Spending Elder).

To see how Mosaic works in practice, let's imagine we've been hired to make a TV commercial to launch a new brand of mid-strength lager. Lager is a fairly utilitarian product. There is little real difference between any of the brands in the market, all of them use the same basic ingredients and brewing process and all taste roughly the same. Success is entirely a question of either branding or price.

A fairly straightforward brief, one might imagine, so no need to overcomplicate things. First, our research shows that German and Czech beer are regarded as the best, so we give ours a vaguely central European sounding name like Karviná Pils (and put 'brewed under license in the UK' in small print on the label). Next we start to think about the advert. If we were contestants on *The Apprentice*, we might immediately conclude that all we have to do is film a couple of blokes – New Urban Colonists, naturally – down the pub, enjoying a couple of 'refreshing' pints of lager beer and saying how great it tastes. Isn't it as simple as that?

Actually it isn't. Lager is consumed in huge quantities, yes it's true, but despite the fact that the product itself is fairly generic (and if you don't believe me, try doing a blind tasting with four or five lagers and see how many you identify successfully) there is a huge number of brands competing for mind and mouth share.

So let's start with the product itself. Well that's the easy bit. Without a good product there's no point in trying to take it to market at all, but lager is lager, so in this category with so few ingredients it's difficult to come up with a bad one. Our lager's strength will determine whether we aim it at the volume end (against brands like Carling, Carlsberg, Fosters, and Castlemaine) where things are fairly generic and pricing is key, or at the premium end (Cruz Campo, Heineken, Becks, Peroni et al) where things are a bit more brand-led and pricing is slightly less of an issue.

After this, things start getting complicated. For example, are we prioritising the pub or the home market? Bottles have a better profile than cans, so do we do one or the other? Or both? How will we position Karviná Pils? Among the continental lagers? Against the lighter American brewskis? With the weaker UK beers? Alongside the exotic Asian labels or the quirky Latin American brands? Will Karviná Pils be available on draft? What kind of outlets should it be available in – traditional boozers or trendy high-street bars? Can we persuade landlords to stock it? Who will drink it? Young males? Middle-aged men? Maybe we should aim it at women? In that case, have we got the right name? In fact how do we know if Karviná Pils is an appropriate name to use? What should the packaging look like…

Before we can launch our beer, we need to find out the answer to all these questions – and several dozen more – because if we get just one of them wrong, our product will be one of the 80 percent that fails to find a market, fails to make an emotional connection and, finally, just fails altogether. To even get this far can take years of product and brand development, but for the purposes of our launch, let's just say that the research has been done and we know we have to target males between the ages of 18 and 24 who usually drink Becks Vier, Staropramen and Amstel. The research also tells us that this group likes beers that are relatively bland with very little flavour, so we decide that the word 'smooth' is a positive way to express this preference.

With this tighter brief it's clear that the original ad idea won't pass muster, but even if it did, there are very strict laws concerning the advertisement and promotion of alcohol that we need to be aware of. We can't have anyone in their late teens featuring in our advert, because we might be perceived as encouraging under-age drinking. For the same reason we can't create an animated character, or contain any references to popular or youth culture. Secondly, the younger target age group is aspirational and will not respond to images of their peers as well as they will to images of the older males they desire to be. Lynx is the UK's best selling men's deodorant. The average age of a Lynx user is 14, yet nowhere in the advertising will you see anybody under the age of 22. Nor can we show people benefitting in any way from the product – if we imply they are funnier, or more attractive to women, or function better after a pint of our lager, our ad will be banned instantly, wasting hundreds of thousands of pounds in the process. In fact even if we imply the beer tastes nice we're on shaky ground, as it could then be argued that we are encouraging binge drinking, which is also forbidden.

It sounds like mission impossible, but in fact there's still a great deal we can do, thanks to our love of concepts and brands and our innate ability to make strong links between seemingly unrelated, abstract ideas.

In the early stages, the Mosaic data can really help us to ensure we know what sort of things will engage our audience. It's not that Mosaic directs what we will do, rather that it informs us. That's the thing to remember about research; it can never tell you what to end up with, but it can show you the right place to start from.

The research reveals two negative things about our audience. First, they tend to be tremendously judgemental, and secondly, quite a few of our target categories are likely to be quite homophobic (Tower Block Living, Conservative Values etc). For that reason two blokes down the pub might send out the wrong message. Nor can we have a bloke drinking on his own, because who on earth aspires to be Billy No-Mates? Nor will two blokes and a girl (Town Gown Transition) work because the audience won't be able to work out the relationship in our 30-second commercial – they might think something a bit weird is going on sexually. That's why most beer commercials go for three blokes (we could throw in a City Adventurer). Four looks like a gang and might seem a bit threatening. We could go for three white mates, down the pub, having a chat about…oh dear! We could run the risk of straying dangerously close to *Daily Mail* reader territory (which surprisingly, is not a Mosaic category, but feels like it ought to be).

In the end we decide to go for two couples (Cultural Leaders with Settled Minority partners) and a friendly barman (Affluent Blue Collar) but not too friendly (Sepia Memories) or too young (University Challenge) or too good looking (Metro Multi-culture) or too unattractive (White Van Culture).

This is the kind of effort required to convince us that something essentially the same is actually something fresh and new. It isn't just true for beer – it is the case for every new product. But even now, our work is not yet done. There's one thing left to do and it's the most difficult challenge of all. Even though we know we can create an ad campaign that will resonate with our target market when they get an opportunity to see it, how do we actually make sure that they take notice? In other words, how do we ensure that we're in the tiny minority of those 3,000 messages a day that doesn't get filtered out? And if we want our campaign to be really successful, it isn't enough to make sure we're not ignored, we need it to be noticed and talked about and acted upon.

In the final chapter of his breakthrough 1976 book *The Selfish Gene*, Richard Dawkins explores a concept he calls a meme, by applying evolutionary theory to the spread of ideas and other cultural phenomena. Dawkins' contention is that memes work like genes. In the way that genes are merely vehicles that allow the transference of biological information, memes are vehicles for the transference of ideas. A meme can be identified as an idea or belief that is transmitted from one person or group to another. He cites jingles, catchphrases, popular songs and even technical ideas such as building arches as examples of memes.

When I read the book as a naïf undergraduate, this part really did strike a chord. So much so that the idea stayed with me for many years, but it was only when I started working in the field of communications that I realised what an excellent observation Dawkins had made. Like genes, memes are subject to mutation as they are passed around, but unlike their biological counterparts, it is possible to pass memes in any direction. They can lie dormant for many years (like an album or movie that finds a new audience years after its release) but are ultimately spread as a result of the behaviour they elicit in their hosts. Marketers are well aware of how memes work; they are often described as 'ideas viruses' or 'contagious thoughts'. Author Malcolm Gladwell describes them as: 'An idea that behaves like a virus... that moves through a population, taking hold in each person it infects.'

What our advert is lacking, then, is a hook that will draw people in and a meme that will ensure that our key information gets passed on. This is not a challenge peculiar to advertisers: it's one that everybody trying to communicate with us faces. One strategy, especially favoured by newspapers and magazines, is to find the broadest entry point for a story – however tenuous – with the aim of drawing in as many people as possible. So a report about a plane crash or terrorist explosion will always lead with the number of British casualties, while people stories will always peg the individual concerned to the biggest brand possible. Thus any story concerning the actor Leslie Grantham will always be headlined with the words '*Eastenders*' Dirty Den', even though he hasn't been in the show for several years. In stories where celebrities are involved, more is always more, which can lead to a ludicrous snowball effect. For example, an anodyne picture of Anne Robinson with an unknown architect, David Collins, taken at a charity launch, is spiced up for consumption for *Daily Mail* readers with the headline: 'The Romantic Link? Anne Robinson's Secret Dates with Madonna's Interior Designer'.

This technique doesn't necessarily require people and it can work for any story. A fairly dull art-history piece, revealing that a new digital scan of the Mona Lisa shows some additional detail in the background of the picture, can achieve lead story status by simply adding the headline: 'The real-life Da Vinci Code: Art historian claims to have unlocked the mystery of Mona Lisa's identity'. Readers expecting to discover the identity of Jesus' living descendants would have been sorely disappointed. We discover instead that the painting 'may reveal' a bridge that 'might have' once spanned the river Trebbia. Even this rather prosaic speculation seems unlikely, as the article concludes with a quote from a sceptical art historian who says:

> The portrait is almost certainly of [Italian noblewoman] Lisa del Giocondo, however unromantic and un-mysterious that idea might be. There have been many attempts to identify the landscape as a specific location and I do not find the resemblance to the Bobbio Bridge all that close. I have great reservations about all attempts to find some obscurely hidden meaning in Renaissance works of art.

The only reason the story ran at all was because the writer could peg it to *The Da Vinci Code*, which is one of the biggest selling books of modern times and therefore judged to be of interest to a significant proportion of the paper's readers.

Although this strategy succeeds in drawing people in, there is little chance of the reader passing the idea on, as there is no meme to reward their engagement. For a newspaper or magazine, whose content has already been paid for by the time readers consume it, this is not an issue, because its job is done once we've bought the publication. Glossy men's and women's magazines are masters of this art. A cover photo featuring a major movie or music star will inevitably have a suggestive strap line along the lines of: 'Gwynnie Naked. Paltrow as you have never heard her before on Sex, Drugs and Rock 'n' Roll.'

Once bought, we turn straight to the interview expecting a salacious insight into a celebrity life. Instead we discover that Gwyneth says she has never done drugs (Drugs – tick); thinks fans are going to like her husband's new album (Rock 'n' Roll – tick); and went to a convent school where sex education was not part of the curriculum (Sex – tick). The remaining 2,000 words are about maybe a recent skiing holiday in the Algarve, a book she's reading about brogues, cupping or something else just as interesting.

Back to our advert then. The key learning point is that we can draw people into our product by pegging it to something they are already familiar with ('Here's something you already love… And look! It's linked to something new and exciting that you're going to love too!'), but we need to ensure they can take something away from the advert too – we still need a meme that they can pass on.

Unless they have developed a brilliant creative idea like the Cadbury gorilla – and brilliant creative ideas like the Cadbury gorilla a) don't come along very often and b) require a marketing director with balls of steel to sign them off – then at this point, many brands will try to involve a celebrity. Ideally the celebrity will be somebody whose values can be aligned with the brand you're trying to promote and somebody whose endorsement you can afford. Celebrity endorsement does not come cheap. The research might tell you Jonathan Ross will go down a storm with the target audience, but for a product like our lager, the budget is unfortunately only likely to stretch to Paul Ross.

The best thing to do is to try and get somebody who's on the way up; somebody whose profile is likely to improve over the course of the endorsement and who might even be persuaded to see our sponsorship as an opportunity. In the end we decide to hire an exciting and edgy, up-and-coming comedian – let's call him Howard Russell – who is starting to make regular appearances on a raft of TV panel shows. Our contract means he'll appear in our commercial and, in return, we'll sponsor his next UK tour, which will give us more opportunity to create a brand alignment between the beer and the man.

Howard is definitely the kind of guy our audience can relate to. He's smart, funny, and good looking in a non-threatening way. Research shows that our audience thinks he looks like he could be a good laugh on a night out and they can relate to his style of observational comedy – it makes them feel like his life is very similar to theirs (even though he's making a living talking to strangers in 8000-seat arenas for £100K a night, while they're working in an office). In order to create a meme, what we need to do is ensure that Howard Russell becomes synonymous with our product. If we succeed the rewards are vast, because every time people see the celebrity, they will think of our brand, in the way that John Lydon = Country Life butter or in the way that teetotallers like Jack Dee and Peter Kaye came to epitomise John Smith's bitter. The creative execution is all-important; everything can still fall apart – expensively – if we get that part wrong.

Back in the mid 90s, I was head of European PR for Actua Sports, a popular range of video games for the original Sony PlayStation. The brand's flagship title was a genuinely groundbreaking game called *Actua Soccer*. Not only was it the first football game to appear on the, then newly launched, Sony

PlayStation and the first one to make proper use of the new console's sound capabilities, with an authentic live commentary (by *Match of the Day*'s Barry Davies and Trevor Brooking), but it was also the first ever football game in 3D. Despite this pedigree, *Actua Soccer* was not the only football game in town. Just like today, the heavyweight champion of the genre was the behemoth of all video games franchises: *FIFA Soccer*.

Launched in 1995, the initial version of *Actua Soccer* performed really well. Reviews and sales were excellent and the game gave the all-conquering *FIFA* a run for its money, taking its publisher EA Sports somewhat by surprise. Despite this success, for the 1997 follow-up, *Actua Soccer 2*, we realised we were going to have to do something special to remain competitive: could we surprise EA a second time?

Across the hall from the PR department was Actua Sports' marketing team. There was something of a rivalry between the two camps. The Head of Marketing felt that his own area of expertise, with its jargon, diplomas and professional qualifications, was a decidedly more intellectual endeavour than public relations, and was keen to make this point as loudly and often as possible. He may have been right, but it's also true to say that the rest of the company thought that most of his department's ideas were rubbish. And most rubbish of all was the TV campaign it devised to launch *Actua Soccer 2*.

To be fair, there was nothing wrong with the main ingredient. Credit where it's due, Marketing had secured the endorsement of a top footballer, Alan Shearer. At that time, Shearer was the current PFA Player of the Year, a star striker for England and Newcastle United and widely regarded to be the greatest English player for a generation. His involvement had cost over £250,000 and the challenge now, for both Marketing and ourselves, was to try to make Shearer synonymous with *Actua Soccer*. In that respect we were not just competing with his club and national team, but his other sponsors as well: McDonald's, Braun and Umbro.

Our contract allowed for a very limited number of press interviews, but the PR team did manage to get pictures of him in an Actua Sports shirt on the front cover of several football and video games magazines. All that we needed now was a killer TV campaign that would cement his affinity with our brand. The ad was of paramount importance, so our incumbent agency was fired, and the brief was awarded to a creative powerhouse from London called Walsh Trott Chick Smith.

Despite a great deal of interest from the rest of the company, the ad was filmed in secrecy. Once it was finally finished, just days before it was to be broadcast to the nation, the PR team was invited into the boardroom, with much pomp and ceremony, to see the result of weeks of effort. It was the centrepiece of a multi-million pound campaign that was going to propel Britain's *Actua Soccer* into the stratosphere and knock *FIFA Soccer* off its smug Canadian perch.

Unfortunately, I don't have a copy of the advert – or, to give it its full title, *Real Football In Your Hands* – which is a shame, because for me it remains, after all these years, the best example of how to get everything wrong that I have ever seen.

Fortunately for us, though, the creative concept is very easy to explain. The 30-second film features a wordy voiceover by comedian Paul Tonkinson, who uses a lot of alliteration to describe the features of the game ('super-smooth soccer skills' – that sort of thing) some of which are a bit technical (would you know, for example, what on earth 'real world physics' is?).

While this is going on, at the bottom of the screen there is a scroll bar containing a list of all the review scores that *Actua Soccer* had received in the specialist games magazines (typically represented as percentages). For the uninitiated, these magazines had confusingly similar names: *PlayStation Pro*, *PlayStation Power*, *PowerStation*, *PlayStation Plus*, *PlayStation Zone*, *PlayStation Magazine*, *Play*, *PlayStation Now*. Indeed one wondered whether many people would know that they were magazines at all, imagining rather that we were playing some kind of word association game.

The central creative concept itself is a pastiche of the Mystery Guest round from BBC's long-running quiz show *A Question of Sport*. Set in a living room, footage of the game itself is interspersed with extreme close-up shots of the gamer. We see fingers, a nose, an ear, some hair, lips, the left eye… who could it be? With five seconds to go, the player scores a goal, the camera pulls back to reveal it is… Ta-dah! None other than Alan Shearer, who leaps out of the chair to celebrate, with a great big cheesy grin and thumbs aloft. The image freezes and Tonkinson delivers the pay-off: 'Actua Soccer 2. Real football in your hands!'

Silence.

'Seriously, what do you think?' asked one of the product managers, as we were leaving the room.

'Well,' I replied. 'I think what we've done here is paid £250,000 to have the most famous footballer in the world star in our TV ad and then gone to great lengths to disguise the fact that it's actually him for 25 of the 30 seconds he's on screen. That's what I think.'

Then I went back to my desk to have a little cry.

For our Karviná Pils commercial, we ensure that we avoid the *Real Football In Your Hands* pitfall by making sure we have our celebrity in shot the whole time. The script has our couples acting out a gag that, although entirely unrelated to the product, is something that might well get talked about.

We join our couples while they are sitting in a bar, obviously taking part in a pub quiz.

An unseen quizmaster breaks the silence, 'Number 12. What is the capital of Belarus?'

None of our team knows the answer. Then Howard has an idea, he nudges his mate and, with a cheeky wink, whispers, 'Use your phone.'

The mate is seen furtively tapping the phone, as if he's looking something up on Google or Wikipedia. Then, at the last moment, he puts the phone to his ear and shouts into it loudly enough for the whole pub to hear, 'Hey Dave, do you know what the capital of Belarus is?'

Then we cut to a pack shot and a voiceover that says, 'Not everything in life is as smooth as a Karviná Pils.'

This treatment ticks all the boxes. No one can argue that it makes our characters look good, and we've made no claims for the product other than to suggest smoothness is a sought-after quality in a lager. They even fail to profit from their playful attempt at cheating. There's always the chance that the client won't like it, so we task one of our researchers to find some suitable alternative jokes on the Internet which we can change a bit to avoid any copyright issues.

Fast-forward a few months, and let us imagine that our campaign has proven to be a huge success. Our achievement is that we have succeeded in convincing people that Karviná Pils is not just another lager, but an exciting new experience; a great long drink to unwind with after a hard day at work and the perfect beverage for a great night out. A new brand will appear on pumps and on bottles in bars and off-licences up and down the country. Bright young things will express their individuality en masse, by choosing Karviná Pils ahead of all other brands, for genuine emotional reasons, because we have succeeded in getting our brand to speak to them and persuaded them to pass our meme on to their family and friends. We can chalk up another success for Everything Now.

And if that sounds facetious, then I apologise; it's not meant to, but now do consider this. Honestly, how many of your opinions do you think are the sum of your own experience, research and analysis? And how many are just the result of you being infected by a meme virus?

We have seen that the kind of 'prevailing wisdom', so common in media reporting, is easy to turn out and rarely challenged. This is ultimately why it prevails. We are told it's important to have an opinion and compelled to take a view. Failing to do so makes you appear uninformed or out of touch. What do you think of Andy

Murray? Nuclear power? Levi's jeans? The conflict in the Middle East? Polish builders? You must have an opinion. But don't worry if you don't – here's a meme we made earlier: you can pass it off as your own.

Yet precisely because this wisdom is so shallowly held, it is so easy to challenge. In November and December of 2010 Britain witnessed the heaviest snowfall and lowest temperature for more than 100 years. 'Why is it that other countries seem to manage while the UK grinds to a standstill?' went the prevailing wisdom, heard time and time again in bars and restaurants, schoolyards and workplaces, on radio and TV or read in newspapers and online reports.

The truth is that any country in the world receiving a 100-year record level of snowfall would find it pretty difficult to manage. I have spent a few Decembers and Januarys working in Helsinki, Olso and Stockholm, during which I experienced plenty of disruptions due to bad weather. The biggest difference was that people in those countries just seemed to moan about them a lot less than the British.

At one point during the 2010 cold snap, somebody said to me, quite angrily, 'Why is it that all these countries with less money than us seem to cope with the snow much better than we do?'

I asked, 'Like where?'

And he replied, 'I don't know.'

If you listen to somebody who does know what they are talking about – a real expert, rather than a presenter or journalist – the effect can be inspiring. Brian Cox, a quantum physicist at the CERN research facility in Switzerland, has become one of the most popular figures on television, especially with children. He might have boy-band good looks (literally, in his case, as he used to be in one) and an easy manner in front of the camera, but the fact that he's rarely talking about anything less complex than Einstein's General Theory of Relativity, superconductors or Schrödinger's cat demonstrates that when a credentialed expert, with an obvious passion for their field, is talking, it's almost always interesting.

If you want to avoid infection by a meme virus, then it pays to remember that people dispensing advice don't necessarily know what they are talking about. Everything Now has led us by our emotions to the belief that the world has been designed to do nothing less than celebrate our individuality: that it is a place where we can achieve our potential as human beings; where we can speak our minds, in the knowledge that our voices will be heard, our concerns addressed and our needs satisfied; where we can do what we choose. Yet the reality is quite different, because despite what we might think, the world is not here exclusively for our benefit. Everything Now provides us with a narrow set of options in a myriad of packages – whether it's products, opinions or ideas – ignorant of the fact we are individually living out almost identical lives.

Part 4: Happiness

Happiness *noun*

State of mind or feeling characterised by contentment, love, satisfaction, pleasure, or joy.

Chapter 15
Happiness

'The pain I feel today is the happiness I had before. That's the deal.' – *C.S. Lewis, author*

Given the choice, what would you rather have: more time or more money?

It's a question that vexes a large number of people (at the time of writing, it has been asked 313,000 times according to Google). The obvious answer is that it depends on your situation – the 'bum in the gutter' and Roman Abramovich representing either end of a scale onto which we all fit, albeit bunched much closer toward the 'bum' end of things – yet year in, year out, surveys are published which suggest that it's free time that we value more.

I am rather sceptical of the results of these surveys for a number of reasons. Firstly, they tend to be devices employed to drive PR and in that respect one should expect the results to be more self-serving than scientific. A survey commissioned by a travel agent, for example, might conclude that we don't feel that we are spending enough time on holiday. The question is also loaded: responding that you need more time can make you sound industrious but philosophical, while saying you want more money can make you sound greedy or materialistic. Some people will say time because it makes them sound better, whether it's true or not. I believe the reality is that most of us would like more of both, because we believe that having more of them will make us happier.

As we have seen, Everything Now is brilliant at disguising contradictions. It appeases our demands for convenience, choice and individuality, by giving us a limited number of very similar propositions that are packaged and positioned in a huge number of different ways. The same is true when it comes to our demands for more time and money. As consumers, Everything Now promises us time in return for money; as workers it promises us money in return for time. Thus is created a vicious circle in which Everything Now ends up becoming the biggest drain upon both: it is both the cause of, and solution to, our time and money worries at the same time.

Everything Now does not come cheap, and in order to afford it, we are required to put the hours in. Over the past 30 years the UK has insidiously developed a culture of working longer and longer hours. In 2010, British workers put in an average 43.7 hours per week; in Europe the average was only 40.4. Nearly 4 million people were working more than 48 hours, with 1 in 25 men working at least a 60-hour week. All this is going on, despite the European Working Time Directive of 1998, which introduced a maximum working week of 48 hours. Overwork forces people into unhealthy lifestyles as the reconciliation between employment and domestic responsibilities becomes incredibly difficult to achieve. Up to 50 percent of UK parents are unhappy with their work and family balance. Over half of British employees reported that work dominated their lives, and that their personal life suffered as a result. Working long hours also leads to increased levels of stress, resulting in irritability, exhaustion and depression.

The situation in the US, the most advanced economy in the world (and thereby the most extreme example of Everything Now) is even worse. Many US workers don't bother taking vacations, even though they are entitled to them. The majority who keep working do so due to concerns about job security, and of those who do manage to get away, almost 70 percent find they can't slow down quickly enough to de-stress adequately whilst they are on holiday. Around one in three check in with work each day. The US also has the lowest number of paid vacation days in the industrialised world, with just 13 on average, compared with 42 days in Italy, 37 in France and 35 in Germany.

Working mothers face a dilemma of trying to keep on top of things in both the home and the workplace. Academic studies continually show these demands are not imagined but, rather, expected of them. A new study finds that women with husbands who work long hours have less time for their own careers as they are the ones who attend to the housework and childcare. A woman is 51 percent more likely to quit her job if her husband works a 60-hour week; among professional women this figure rises to 112 percent.

Long hours affect all dual-earner families, but workers in professional and managerial occupations are particularly affected, because it is within this group that the culture of overwork and intensive parenting tends to be most pronounced. The costs of assistance – in the form of cleaners, home-helpers, nannies, or child-minders – can be prohibitively expensive. This expenditure is not tax deductible and mothers can end up working simply to cover the costs of hired help.

Social mores also mean that striking a decent work-life balance is profoundly difficult. In a world where everyone appears to be rushing around at 100 miles an hour, admitting to spending a lazy morning in bed or chilling out in front of the PlayStation is frowned upon. Admit to doing so and comments like 'Well, I wish I had the time to...' are what you will usually hear. We wear our industry like badges of honour, 'I've been too busy to even think about a holiday...', and use it as a handy excuse, 'Sorry I've not got back to you, but I've been snowed under...'.

We might feel that earning a good living can provide good living, but few of us discover that we can buy ourselves happiness. This situation couldn't be any further away from the technological promises of the 1960s and 70s, when it was believed that we would work six-hour days and four-day weeks in paperless offices as robots worked tirelessly in the permanent night of windowless factories producing the consumer goods we would need to maximise our surfeit of leisure time.

The impact of the technological revolution has been just as significant as everyone imagined: it is the implications that have proven to be wildly inaccurate. Technology tends to be labour changing as much as it is labour saving. It's impossible to imagine office life before desktop computers, smartphones, email and constant Internet access, so much so, that an office scene as recent as 1990 would look like something straight out of a quaint period drama. Technological devices, communications and other innovations have undoubtedly changed the workplace, but they haven't reduced the workload.

These pressures have impacted the way we spend what little free time we have. Brands do provide an emotional outlet, it's true, but they can also make us feel that we are able to buy ourselves more time. Many products are presented as a shortcut, albeit one that is little more than notional in practice. 'No time to cook for yourself? Why not try one of our freshly prepared, Artisan Ready Meals.' It might be four times the price of the raw ingredients, but if you're willing to suspend your disbelief and ignore the juxtaposition of packaging that promises gourmet quality and a plastic tray containing heavily processed food that has been mass produced on an industrial scale – and don't stop to question the usefulness of the phrase 'freshly prepared' – then you might believe that you're eating in a top restaurant. One that's having an off day. And where the chef has phoned in sick. And the cooker's broken, so the pot-washer has had to step in and microwave everything. Enjoy!

The ability to buy everything from a single retailer similarly offers a notional shortcut, but again expediency is not incontrovertibly conducive to happiness. The fact that the town centre high street is in sharp decline is a cause of consternation for many people. I believe the situation is probably terminal, and I expect we will see more and more specialist retailers disappear over the next few years. The generalists that remain will in turn look for bigger and bigger stores: the kind that can be found in purpose-built shopping centres and retail parks on the edges of town.

For centuries, UK towns and cities have had shops and markets in the centre. Even today retail is usually the most significant component of urban regeneration schemes. This is largely because the popularity of retail makes it the best way of attracting people into the heart of the city. As anyone who's queued in bank holiday traffic at a shopping centre or IKEA-style megastore will testify, retailers attract people. Lose the retailers from our urban centres and they lose the means of attracting visitors: in effect our towns and cities will lose their hearts.

There is no Plan B for what we might use our city centres for instead. All the bright ideas for mixed-use schemes involving business, residential and leisure contain a significant retail component. If the developers cannot attract an anchor retailer, there is inevitably no scheme. Some of our biggest cities have spent a decade trying – and failing – to deliver city centre retail-led developments. Schemes like Sevenstone and The Moor in Sheffield, Eastgate in Leeds and WestQuay in Southampton have all been designed to boost local economies and provide opportunities for residents and visitors, but when, and in some cases whether, they will be delivered is unclear. We have to accept that we may be drifting toward a US civic model, where life is conducted at the periphery of urban centres in purpose-built malls and leisure parks, and the city centre itself is either a don't-go or a no-go area.

Retail Therapy may not be the answer for our city centres, but there is little evidence that it is in any way therapeutic for the individual either. The fact is that accruing material possessions doesn't necessarily make you happier. A 2010 study of 32,000 young people, by the National Foundation for Educational Research, concluded that children living in poverty are just as happy as their wealthier classmates. The survey showed that wealth has very little influence over children's well-being when compared to things like how often they eat a meal with family or friends, how much contact time they have with their parents and siblings, whether they can talk to their parents about their worries, and whether or not they have a close friend or two.

Tom Benton, the report's main author, said:

> If we are interested in the happiness and well-being of young people we need to look beyond how much money they have.
>
> In particular, growing up in a supportive and safe environment, both within the home and elsewhere appear to be far more important. Parents making the effort to spend time with their children are a major positive influence on their chances of being happy.

Rather than making us happier, Everything Now appears to be having the opposite effect. In April 2009 as part of his Easter message, the Archbishop of Canterbury, Dr Rowan Williams, called for a less angry British society. He identified Everything Now culture as the primary cause:

> We are able to remember for a moment that even in a society where everyone seems to be insanely focused on getting and winning, there are times when we need to stand still and just face ourselves quietly.
>
> We've had a few decades of being told we have a right to get whatever we want – cash, status, pleasure. Fair enough, if what's been normal before is oppression and unfairness. Not so sensible if what it means is a system that sets everyone against everyone else and tells us we can be as angry as we like if we don't get exactly what we think we want.

The UK has the worst incidence of road rage in the world, bar South Africa (which, given the high incidence of drive-by shootings, is way out in front). A third of us are not on speaking terms with our neighbours, and five percent have actually had a fight with the person living next door. Levels of violence in the workplace are also increasing. Problems associated with work-related violence are nothing new, but the causes are changing. In the past, the most common cause was the action of an outsider – robberies and other attacks perpetrated by criminals. In recent years, the violence has often resulted from disputes involving co-workers, ex-workers and angry clients or customers. A total of 8,746 acts of violence against NHS staff were reported in 2008. 27 percent of nurses have been attacked at work. Attacks on teachers are also on the rise. In 2007, there were 7,306 reports of physical or verbal attacks on teachers; 4,608 of these involved physical violence.

We are bringing up a generation that expects to be able to have what they want and for things to go their way. When they don't, the result is frustration and anger. These emotions are inevitable, because while the contradictions in Everything Now are disguised, they are still there: an inherent part of everyday life.

The basis of Everything Now is emotional not rational: it addresses wants not needs. That is why it cannot provide us with actual happiness. It responds to the fact that we want happiness by providing us with conceptual shortcuts and distractions, but these propositions can never satisfy our fundamental need. Yet, rather than reject Everything Now for this failure, we return to it again and again in search of further, fruitless solutions. The cycle results in an increasingly homogenised society, with fewer and fewer genuine alternatives open to us. We live in different houses that have similar laminate floors and magnolia walls. We watch the same programmes on different plasma TVs. We eat the same processed food in the guise of different ready meals. We express our individuality by listening to similar music by different artists and wearing different clothes made by the same brands.

We work long hours, in different offices using the same computer software to send variations of the same report (a working day of 'Ctrl A: Ctrl C: Ctrl V: Ctrl P'); or on different building sites; constructing similar developments, or in different factories creating similar products. We spend our free time in different shopping centres, buying similar goods from similar retailers. We take different holidays in different locations, but in similar sun-drenched resorts where everybody speaks the same language as ourselves. We hold similar, unique opinions, voice similar personal concerns, vote for different political parties who all have similar centre-right ideologies. We enjoy different nights out at similar bars and clubs and post similar photos on different Facebook pages.

Everything Now has brought us some tangible benefits. Our living standards have improved dramatically over the past 50 years; higher education and global travel, once privileges enjoyed by few, are now just rights of passage for many young people; and we are healthier, better fed, watered, cared for, educated and entertained than any generation in history. But we are not happier.

As a nation we are no more content than we were during the years of post-war austerity, when want was genuine. The contradictions of Everything Now are making us angrier, more uptight, more dissatisfied, more frustrated and more tired. The main source of happiness remains human relationships, which have been sacrificed to a large extent in order to support the economic growth that is needed to pay for the materialism and convenience of Everything Now.

We don't need anything, but as long as we keep being shown what we can spend our money on, we keep on spending. And that is how Everything Now is sustained: by giving us more of the things we don't need. It used to be enough to have a family car and a family home; but many people are not satisfied with one house, they want two, while a car has become a common 18th birthday present. We need to change these goals and values, because if you are driven by achieving fame and fortune you are unlikely to be satisfied whatever level of wealth or notoriety you achieve.

There is one final irony, but it is undoubtedly the biggest. The UN estimates we are currently using 1.4 times more resources than the earth can sustain. Whatever your views are on climate change, our reliance on fossil fuels, the rapid expansion of the world's population, the challenges of food supply, we can surely agree that this statistic contains the human race's most significant challenges of the next 40 years. A study, published in January 2011 by the UK's Institution of Mechanical Engineers, suggested we might be in possession of the solution, as it revealed that we already have all the tools at our disposal to cope with a global population of nine billion people. The report said:

> There is no need to delay action while waiting for the next greatest technical discovery or breakthrough idea on population control…[There are] no insurmountable technical issues in meeting the basic needs of nine billion people… sustainable engineering solutions largely exist.

For example, switching to a supply of sustainable low-carbon energy does not require some scientific breakthrough as many people think – or even any more research at all – it is entirely possible using existing technologies. Furthermore, there is no need for any of the earth's projected 2050 population of 10 billion to starve or for us to ruin the environment in the process of trying to feed them. A target of 3,000 calories per person per day is an entirely realistic yield, even as farms take steps to protect the environment by reducing reliance on fossil fuels and calling a halt to deforestation.

But just because we have the technology doesn't mean that we will use it. What holds us back are economic and political pressures. The short-termism of Everything Now prevents the adoption of existing technologies such as nuclear power or concentrated solar energy, and its wastefulness means that over a third of all food that is harvested is simply thrown away.

These issues are too important to brush aside as 'Market Failures'. We need to put pressure on our politicians and economists to deliver change, and we must be prepared to support them when they do, even when the benefits may not be realised for decades to come. The concept of waiting has become anathema to us, but we must relearn how to be patient, because if we continue to have Everything Now today, there might well be nothing left for us tomorrow.

Epilogue
Wait Here

Shortly after completing *Everything Now*, I was invited to talk at
the Annual Conference of Labour Management Intelligence. My
brief was to provide an employer's perspective on 'issues affecting
employment and skills' in the Creative Content Industries.

Whilst reviewing my presentation I was also listening to Spotify,
a music streaming service that epitomises Everything Now, by
pretty much giving you everything now (at least as far as music is
concerned). Simply type the name of a song or artist into Spotify
and, unless you're so left-field in your music taste that you've
disappeared over the horizon, you will find it there, instantly, ready
to play. It is like having an infinite CD collection, but one that is
meticulously catalogued and provided free of charge (you'll never
find a case without a CD in it either). All you are required to do,
in return for listening to whatever you want, is put up with an
occasional advert, played every four songs or so. Nothing could
be more convenient.

Spotify is undeniably useful in many respects. Certainly I find
it much easier to find what I'm looking for there than I do by
rifling through my own haphazardly indexed music collection.
I'll also concede that back in the day, when I was a music-
obsessed teenager and access to the music I loved was rationed
parsimoniously, the very thought of an on-demand service such
as this would have made me go weak at the knees, like a beggar
at a banquet. Yet despite all these obvious benefits, I don't really
like Spotify and here's why.

As far as my relationship with music goes, convenience is not
really an issue. Spotify is all well and good as a short cut to old

favourites – no need to wonder where I put that copy of Joy Division's *Unknown Pleasures* any more – but I do already own those recordings anyway. Getting up out of my chair to find something to play is not a major source of irritation. For my part the most joyful aspect of my interest in music is the journey of discovery. Occasionally I'll hear a song for the first time and it will spark something inside me – just like the brands, making one of their ephemeral emotional connections. I will decide that I like it and maybe pay enough attention to catch the name of the artist. Perhaps I like it so much that I'm persuaded to investigate further, investing in the purchase of an album. And, because I've paid for it, I'll also invest the time to listen to it. Over the course of several plays it grows on me, and now I start to really like it. Maybe I decide to see the band live or perhaps just want to find out more about them. I might even investigate a few previous releases. There are so many roads to follow on the journey from first listen to fan.

Or at least there were. Today if you hear a song you like, simply type the artist's name into Spotify and you will be brought, instantaneously, everything they've ever recorded, helpfully ranked in order of popularity, just to make things easier for you. Please don't misunderstand: I'm no Luddite. Spotify doesn't make me angry, or even pine for the good old days. It might mean that my kids never have the same relationship with music as I have, but what they've never had, they'll never miss, and they also have a lot of great things that I didn't, so the fact they use Spotify is not high on my list of parental concerns. The interesting point is that Spotify, as Everything Now incarnate, highlights the biggest problem of a supply economy: in the long run, who benefits?

In the case of Spotify, it's not the artists. To count all the articles espousing the inability of musicians to make a decent living from sales of recorded music any more would take a very long time. It's not the rights owners either, nor the music publishers or record labels. According to the same articles they are in a worse position than the artists, without revenue from live performances to fall back on, seemingly spending every waking hour writing up then tearing up new business models. Arguably, it's not even Spotify itself, which is still operating at a loss, and failing to persuade punters that unlimited, advert-free access to all the music ever recorded for less than £5 a month is a good deal. And it's certainly difficult to see them coming up with a better offer.

That leaves us then, the listeners like me, happily enjoying Spotify's generous, free, entry-level music service in return for listening to a few anodyne adverts? For now, maybe, but in the long run, I think not. It is difficult to imagine the money generated from these adverts ever replacing the money generated from vinyl and CD sales. Whilst it's true that this money was paying for Elton John's flower and champagne bills, it was also paying for a highly sophisticated filtering and talent-spotting process known as A&R (artist and repertoire). With music, one person's essential sounds are someone else's migraine; but while we might not agree on what we like, we can agree that what we like constitutes a very small part of the whole. The vast majority of Spotify's eight million plus available tracks have never even been played once.

Just as the attempt to increase the public understanding of science opened the door for bad ideas to flourish along with the good, so it has never been easier for a musician to take their music to market: whether or not they should bother is no longer a question. I believe we will come to mourn the passing of these filters – the A&Rs, the radio producers, the music journalists – once the onerous burden of quality control falls squarely on our own shoulders.

We have all heard of the law of supply and demand, but Everything Now is entirely about supply. Nobody ever demanded that eight million songs be made immediately available for free; nobody demanded a Tesco store on every corner; no employer demanded the production of hundreds of thousands of inappropriately trained graduates; nobody demanded that they should have 200 different varieties of soap, toothpaste or yogurt to choose from; and nobody, despite what the CEO of Heinz might say, has ever demanded that beans on toast should be made instantly available. Everything Now does not supply us with the things we want: it supplies us with the things we can be persuaded to want. The solution is simply to demand something different.

And so it was that as I was reviewing my presentation, entitled *Employment and Skills Issues within the Creative Content Industries*, listening to my free version of Spotify, I came to hear an advertisement for the University of Teesside. The first thing that struck me was, given that Spotify knows my age and occupation, perhaps its database management software could do with some debugging, but then something serendipitous happened. The slide under review was headed: *Will Doing This Degree Get Me The Job I Want?* At that moment, the jaunty voiceover invited me to, 'Come and Study at the University of Teesside,' going on to explain, 'We've a range of courses on offer, with everything from Forensic Science to Video Games. The University of Teesside: Inspiring Success!'

Sources

Chapter 1. Everything Now

Purdy, L., 'The Dissatisfaction Syndrome', Publicis May 2002.
Davies, John, 'Debt Facts and Figures July 2011', Credit Action, July 2011
Bott, David, (Director of Innovation Programmes, UK Government Technology Strategy Board), 'Challenge = Opportunity' The 9th Roberts Lecture, University of Sheffield, 18 October 2011
Report Card 7: *Child Poverty in Perspective: An Overview of Child Well-being in Rich Countries*, UNICEF Innocenti Research Centre, September 2007
Children's Well-being in UK, Sweden and Spain: The Role of Inequality and Materialism: A Qualitative Study, UNICEF Ipsos MORI in partnership with Dr Agnes Nairn, June 2011

Chapter 2. We'll tell you what you want, what you really, really want

'Bottled Water UK', Mintel Report, 20 July 2005
Ardagh, J., 'By Popular Demand', The 2011 UK Soft Drinks Report, Zenith International on behalf of the British Soft Drinks Association.
Maslow, A.H., 'A Theory of Human Motivation', *Psychological Review* Vol. 50:4 (1943): 370–96
Smart, John, 'Measuring Innovation in an Accelerating World: Review of "A Possible Declining Trend for Worldwide Innovation",' Acceleration Studies Foundation, 2005
Bott, David, (Director of Innovation Programmes, UK Government Technology Strategy Board), 'Challenge = Opportunity' The 9th Roberts Lecture, University of Sheffield, 18 October 2011

Chapter 3. What Happened to the Future?

Dowling, Tim, 'The Rise and Rise of Convenience Food', *The Guardian*, 19 May 2006

Zemeckis, Robert (Dir.), *Back to the Future Trilogy*, Universal Pictures UK, 25 October 2010

Kennedy, President J.F., Address about the Space Effort, Rice University, 12 September 1962

'A History of the Programme: Eurofighter Typhoon: designed today for future needs' <www.eurofighter.com/eurofighter-typhoon/programme/history.html>

Fearn, Hannah, 'Science Funding Cuts Will Devastate Economy Warns Brian Cox', *Times Educational Supplement*, 21 September 2010

Chapter 4. Available in Magnolia, Vanilla, Cream or Beige

Anderson, Chris, *Free: The Future of Radical Price*, Random House, 2009

Anderson, Chris, *The Long Tail*, Random House Business, 2007

Schwartz, Barry, *The Paradox of Choice*, Ecco, 2003

Iyengar, Sheena S. and Mark R. Lepper, 'When Choice Is Demotivating: Can One Desire Too Much of a Good Thing?', *Journal of Personality and Social Psychology* Vol. 79:6 (2000): 995-1006

A Guide to the Project Management Body of Knowledge, Project Management Pub (4th edition), Jan 2009

Ford, Henry, *My Life and Work*, BN Publishing, 2005

Focus on Consumer Prices, UK National Office of Statistics, October 2010

Girouard, B., Holloman, D., Soares, D., 'Overcoming the Margin Squeeze: Breakthrough Strategies for the Consumer Packaged Goods Industry', Capgemeni, 2006

'40% of UK websites get NO visitors', *Direct Marketing International Magazine*, 19 March 2011

Leisure Outside the Home Market Review 2010, Key Note Publications Ltd, Nov 2010

Chapter 5. Knowledge Without Application

Anderson, Robert, *British Universities Past and Present*, Hambledon Continuum, 2006

Spilsbury, M., L. Giles and M. Campbell, *Ambition 2020: World Class Skills and Jobs for the UK*, UK Commission for Employment and Skills, 2010

Education at a Glance 2008: OECD Indicators, Organisation for Economic Co-operation and Development, 2008

Florida, Richard, *The Rise Of The Creative Class: And How It's Transforming Work, Leisure, Community And Everyday Life*, Basic Books, 2002

Annual Employment Statistics (BRES) 2010 Office of National Satistics

UK Universities League Tables, the *Sunday Times*, 2010

Chapter 6. The Great Unknown

Raymond, Henry J., Editorial, *New York Times*, 26 June 1864

Weber, Jennifer L., *Copperheads: The Rise and Fall of Lincoln's Opponents in the North,* OUP, 2008

Various, *The Public Understanding of Science*, The Royal Society, 1985

Durant, J.R. et al., 'The Public Understanding of Science', *Nature* Vol. 340 (August 1989): 11-14

Realising Our Potential, UK Government White Paper by The Committee for the Public Understanding of Science, 1993

Jay, Emma (Dir.), *Science Under Attack, Horizon* episode, BBC Worldwide, 24 January 2011

Wakefield et al, 'Retraction: Enterocolitis in Children with Developmental Disorders', *The Lancet*, 28 January 2010

Clarkson, Jeremy, *The World According to Clarkson* (Volumes 1-4), Michael Joseph, 2010

Chapter 7. You Can Prove Anything With Facts

Goldacre, Ben, *Bad Science*, Harper Perennial, 2009
Schlosser, Eric, *Fast Food Nation*, Penguin, 2002
Critser, Greg, *Fat Land*, Penguin, 2004
'McDonald's Bigger Big Mac', *Fast Food News*, 15 June 2006
Poulter, Sean, 'McDonald's – Target for Backlash over Junk Food', *Daily Mail*, 27 February 2007
Dawkins, Richard, *The God Delusion*, Bantam Press, 2006
McGrath, Alister and Joanna Collicutt McGrath, *The Dawkins Delusion*, SPCK Publishing, 2007
The O'Reilly Factor, Fox News, 12 October 2009

Chapter 8. The 21 Signs of Ageing

Spilsbury, M., L. Giles and M. Campbell, *Ambition 2020: World Class Skills and Jobs for the UK*, UK Commission for Employment and Skills, 2010
Procter & Gamble Annual Report, 2010
Warrell, David A., Timothy M, Cox and John D, Firth, eds, *Oxford Textbook of Medicine*, OUP, 2010
Anti-ageing Skincare – Europe, Mintel Report, December 2010
Schewe, Phillip F., *The Grid: A Journey Through the Heart of our Electrified World*, National Academic Press, 2006
Conservative Party Manifesto, 2010
Liberal Democrat Party Manifesto, 2010
Labour Party Manifesto, 2010
Dirty Bomb, *Horizon* episode, BBC Worldwide, 2003
Percival, Daniel (Dir.), *Dirty War*, BBC Films, 2004
Fact Sheet on Dirty Bombs, United States Nuclear Regulatory Commission, August 2010
Audette, Derek R., 'Get it Straight! Smoking Does Not Cause Cancer', Audette-O-Blog, 24 October 2005

Chapter 9. Making Your Mind Up

Various, *Daily Mail,* October-December 2009
Keen, Andrew, *The Cult of the Amateur,* Nicholas Brealey Publishing, 2007
Industry Survey: PR in Numbers – The State of the Nation, Chartered Institute of Public Relations Report, November 2005
Welfare Reform Bill, Department for Work and Pensions UK, November 2010

Chapter 10. The Real Thing

Godin, Seth, Seth's Blog, <sethgodin.typepad.com/seths_blog>, 13 December 2009
Yates, Charles, 'Cyril the Swan is Nicked', *The Sun*, 5 October 2001
'The Hartlepool Monkey, Who Hung The Monkey?' <www.thisishartlepool.co.uk>
Hood, Bruce M., and Paul Bloom, 'Children prefer certain individuals over perfect duplicates', Cognition 106 (2008) p455–462
'GALAXY probiotic the UK's first chocolate probiotic drink', *The Grocery Trader*, 10 November 2010
'Fallon and MPC "Go Ape" for Cadbury's Dairy Milk', The Moving Picture Company, Press Release, September 2007
'Brands and Radio Survey', MK Communications Ltd for EMAP Performance, 2004
McClure, Tomlin, Cypert, Montague and Montague, 'Neural Correlates of Behavioural Preference for Culturally Familiar Drinks', *Neuron* Vol. 44 (14 October 2004): 379-87

Chapter 11. Have Your Say. Why Your Opinion Is Important to Us

Davies, Nick, *Flat Earth News*, Chatto & Windus, 2008
Crisell, A., *An Introductory History of British Broadcasting*, Routledge, 2002
Your Call, BBC Radio 5 Live, 16 December 2010
BBC News 24 Channel, 13 December 2010, 14 December 2010

Chapter 12. Making Friends and Influencing People

Richards, Jef I., *Deceptive Advertising: Behavioural Study of a Legal Concept*, Routledge, 1990

Rogers, Everett, *Theory of the Diffusion of Innovations*, Glencoe Free Press, 1963

<www.ABC.org.uk>

Green, Heather, 'The 1% Rule', *Bloomberg Businessweek*, 10 May 2006

'Rage Against the Machine Couple Celebrate "Stratospheric" Chart Campaign', *Metro*, 21 December 2009

Chapter 13. The Empathy Tango

Simmons, John, *Great Brand Stories: Innocent: Building a Brand from Nothing but Fruit*, Cyan Books, 2007

'Start Up Failures: The Real Numbers', StratumLearning, <http://smallbiztrends.com>, 28 April 2008

Barclays Bank, Survey of UK Business Start Ups in 2007, March 2008

Chapter 14. Yes! We Are All Individuals

Hopson, Barrie and Katie Ledger, *And What Do You Do? 10 Steps to creating a Portfolio Career*, A & C Black, 2009

Chapman, Graham, John Cleese, Terry Gilliam, Eric Idle, Terry Jones and Michael Palin, *Monty Python's Life of Brian (of Nazareth)/ MontyPythonScrapbook*, Mandarin, 1979

Blythman, Joanna, *Shopped*, Fourth Estate, 2004

Blythman, Joanna, in interview with Dan Kieran, *The Idler*, Issue 34, December 2004

Mitchell, Alan, *Efficient Consumer Response: A New Paradigm for the European FMCG Sector*, London: FT Retail and Consumer Publishing, Pearson Professional, 1997

Schneider, Joan and Julie Hall, 'Why Most Product Launches Fail', *Harvard Business Review*, April 2011

Wrigley and Lowe, '32 Reading Retail: A Geographic Perspective on Retailing', <www.Andidas.com>, 2002

Mosaic UK 2009, Experian 2009

Dawkins, Richard, *The Selfish Gene*, OUP, 1976

Gladwell, Malcolm, *The Tipping Point: How Little Things Can Make a Big Difference*, Abacus; (Re-issue edition), 2002

'The Romantic Link? Anne Robinson's Secret Date with Madonna's Interior Designer', *Daily Mail*, 20 November 2007

Pisa, Nick, 'The real-life Da Vinci Code: Art historian claims to have unlocked the mystery of Mona Lisa's identity', *Daily Mail*, 10 January 2011.

Chapter 15. Happiness

'Time is more than Money', White and Hutchinson Group Survey, April 2006 (republished September 2010)

Westin Hotels Survey, October 2010

Youngjoo Cha, 'Reinforcing Separate Spheres: The Effect of Spousal Overwork on Men's and Women's Employment in Dual-Earner Households', *American Sociological Review*, April 2010

'Reasons to be Cheerful: Being a 12-year-old Boy who Eats Dinner with his Family', UK Department of Education Survey, December 2010

'Children in Poverty "As Happy as More Affluent Classmates"', *The Guardian*, 23 December 2010

'Population: One Planet, Too Many People', UK Institution of Mechanical Engineers, January 2011

'Foresight Study on World Food and Agricultural Systems in 2050', CIRAD-INRA, January 2011

Acknowledgements

Steve McKevitt would like to thank the following people for their help, support, assistance or any combination thereof:

Ian Daley, Dr Fiona McKevitt, Franklin Carolan, Robson Brearley, Dr Vincent T. Cunliffe, Professor Mike Campbell, Lee Roberts and the rest of the team at Golden.

Steve McKevitt is an expert in marketing, communications and branding. Over a 20 year career, his clients have included Nike, Coca-Cola, Deutsche Bank, Sony PlayStation, Harvey Nichols, Motorola, Universal, Virgin, BT and Atari. His critically acclaimed book *City Slackers* revealed how most corporate business nowadays is actually conducted on the assumption that it will be a failure.

Steve is chairman of Golden, an ideas agency with clients in the UK, Europe and USA. He is married with three children and lives in Yorkshire.

For further information on this book,
and for Route's full book programme
please visit:

www.route-online.com